# 50 Most Popular Jar Cookbook

## Quick and Yummy Breakfast, Lunch and Dinner for Camping, Office, Home & Kids

Learn the Easiest Way to Can Foods with 10 Top Best Canning Recipes

Anna Leigh Robinson

**Autumn Leaf**
PUBLISHING HOUSE

DESIGN & COVER ART

REBECCA WRIGHT

First Edition

# Acknowledgments

This work would not have been possible without the support of two very special people. I want to thank my mother, Martha Jackson, for all her contribution, hard work and dedication to this book project. I am also indebted to my cute daughter, Jennifer Robinson, who helped me write this book.

# Contents

# 1 Feeling Jarred?

"It was the best of times, it was the worst of times..."
Well, I'm not sure if this is the worst, but times right now
are certainly difficult. The pandemic may have ended, as
they say, but we are still dealing with its effects. The
economy of our country as well as other countries, is
trying to bounce back. The political climate of the world is
also not looking too good. And amidst all of these, we still
have to live our lives and make dinner.

Imagine having a rough day at work, coming home, just
wanting to relax, and finding out that you will have to

cook a full-blown meal for yourself, or worse, for the whole family. Buying fast food meals will cost you and is often not good for your body. These hard times have got us saving or cutting back on a lot of things, but something that most people tend to forget about is saving time.

We have been used to managing our time for work so much that we tend to forget to allot time for ourselves and even for food which we need to survive.

That is why I made this book. It's for those people who want to enjoy a good nutritious meal prepared at home for less cash and less time. This is all about meal prepping so that things can be easier to reheat after a busy day.

I really do like using jars, so the whole concept of meal-prepping is appealing to me. I have to prepare a lot for my family, and that's on top of work. I can just cook or prepare a big batch of dishes and stash it away for future consumption, then free up my time with my family.

My meal-prepping sessions during the weekends also contribute to family time since we prepare the food as a family and we put those kids to good use (hey, it's a free and legal form of child labor). Kidding aside, cooking with kids also develops their sense of responsibility and creativity and helps them develop a skill that they will be using in the future by themselves.

So, let's get jarring!

# 2 Kandor-ing Food

When talking about putting food into jars in modern jargon, there are actually two connotations to keep in mind, which the recipes here will be covering. One is the simple storing of food in jars and then placing them in the pantry or fridge, depending on the type of food. While simple, food stored this way will only last for a week or 2, depending on the food and how it was handled. This is a nice way to portion your food items or store ingredients. This is also a good way of taking the amount of food you need and then returning the rest to your storage without them being contaminated—or at least lessening the risks.

The other connotation is canning. Yes, I know we are using jars, but home canners use these mason jars for their long-term storage. If done right, food can last months, even a year, in a properly sealed jar. It may take a bit more work and equipment to properly seal in food, but I think it's worth it considering the extremely long shelf life that you will get, even without the aid of refrigeration.

But why jarred meals? Here are some good points to convince you.

• Glass jars are easy to clean and do not degrade over time, so you may put food in it for a really long time without any fear of contamination. Most plastic containers, particularly those with Bisphenol A (BPA), are known to degrade with exposure to heat and can contaminate their contents. Glass, on the other hand, is made from silicon dioxide, which is non-toxic and non-reactive, so it can handle whatever type of food you put in it.

• Glass is a reusable resource. Plastics are prone to scratching and scraping, which results in smaller plastic particles called microplastics. These may seem harmless at first, but it's one of the major environmental problems scientists around the world are currently trying to solve. They get stored in the digestive tracts of smaller organisms and can transfer to us when we consume them, which can lead to blockages. Glass might be fragile or brittle, but even when broken, it can just be melted down and reformed again into a different glass product—a cycle that can be repeated several times.

- Even if the glass is brittle, properly made mason jars are quite tough, relatively speaking. Just look for ones that are functional, not just the ornamental ones that they use for drinking glasses. Mason jars are made with thicker walls to withstand the high temperatures and pressure that come with pressure canning, which we will discuss later. Since they can withstand a relatively high temperature, they're easy to clean and sanitize—perfect for multiple uses.

- Since they are sturdy, and depending on the type of food you want to store, you can place the jars in the fridge or warm them up in a microwave without breaking. Just don't cool it down and then suddenly heat it up. That's how you get shards of glass in your food.

• Mason jars are actually cheap for something that will last you a long time. You will only have to replace the lid every time you use it for canning, but if you are just storing it in the fridge or pantry for a relatively short time, you can just wash and sanitize the lids and jar rings every time. Other than that, if you take care of them, the jars themselves will last you a lifetime. You can buy them in different sizes for a large batch or for individual servings.

• Speaking of lids and seals, the lid of a mason jar usually comes with a special sealing compound that melts at a certain temperature. This makes it the ideal choice for home canners since the seal makes it airtight and watertight, preserving the contents at a certain temperature and pressure, which prevents the growth of harmful molds and bacteria. When properly sealed, you can store them in your pantry standing up or even lying on their side in the fridge without a problem. Some mason jar brands can even withstand freezing, but you have to carefully check that the brand you are using is capable of it.

• Since mason jars can be closed tightly and are quite compact, you can bring one to your office for lunch or snacks. They are quite heavy, though, so it can add to the strain of commuting, but if you have your own car, then it's not a problem.

# 3 Being Well-Equipped

Now, before you start jamming some oats into a jar, we need to have some equipment ready. Let's do a rundown.

• The first thing you will need is a set of mason jars, of course. They are available at different price points and sizes, but the styles look pretty much the same. Most of the mason jars available today still look the same as they were designed by the great John Mason back in 1858. Look for jars that specify handling heat and pressure, whether you are going to use them for canning or just for regular storage, as these will last longer than ornamental mason jars. The jars used for canning also have airtight lids, making them good for liquids, and can even be used for fermentations. As for the size, 16 oz. jars are the most common, and I think they are perfect for a single meal serving. If you want smaller ones for sauces or spreads, you can get 4 or 8 oz. sizes. If you are looking for bulk storage, you can get a 32 oz. jar.

- Mason jars usually come with a flat lid and a metal ring to secure the lids on. Now, if you are simply going to use the jars for dry storage in the pantry, then these lids are perfectly acceptable. However, if you are looking to perform the canning process, then you will need some extra lids every time you make a new batch. You can buy a set of lids before you start a second batch and for every batch after that. Do not reuse the lids you used for canning since the sealing compound has already melted and will not reform again. As for the metal rings or securing bands, you may replace them as you see fit since they tend to rust after some time. That is why canners tend to remove the band once they are sure that the seal is properly formed.

- Moisture and oxygen are the enemies, particularly if you are using dehydrated foods. Dehydrated foods can last years as long as they do not come into contact with moisture and oxygen. Now, mason jars can provide air-tight seals, but there is the matter of the air already in the jar. You need some special tools and items for this. Both have pros and cons, but you can't go wrong with either one.

o One option is placing an oxygen absorber in the jar with the food. These are small packets that are semi-permeable, commonly filled with iron compounds or activated carbon, which absorb the oxygen in the jar. These are effective, but you will have to replace them after each use. Luckily, they are quite cheap, and you can get them in bulk.

o If you want to invest a bit, you can get a food saver for jars. This is a mechanical pump that sucks the air out of your jars, creating a vacuum. Some models come with their own special lids, which you seal your jars in, while others can be used on regular mason jar lids. Some make use of a small hand pump to manually suck the air out, while more expensive models use an automated pump and can even tell you how strong the vacuum is.

• Canning funnels are also handy whether you are

using the jars for canning or for regular dry storage. The jars actually come with a wide mouth, but sometimes, it's still not enough, and the canning funnel gives you a few extra inches of space to catch whatever it is you are pouring into them, particularly chunky stuff like stews. I suggest a metal or stainless steel canning funnel since it's easier to clean and will need to be boiled for canning. Just choose one that can fit into your jars.

• Other items that you will need are regular utensils for cooking, like knives, cutting boards, ladles, spoons, and others. Any basic American kitchen should be able to get you cooking a number of recipes in this book, but if you feel that your equipment is lacking, you may look for necessary equipment in your local kitchen supply store or borrow some from your neighbors.

# 4 More Than Just Pickles!

Now we come to the recipes. Most of these recipes feature meals in jars to be eaten within the week and stored in the fridge or pantry. You can adjust recipes according to your style and taste if you like. The recipes here are designed more for a weekly meal preparation setting and will last 5 to 7 days in the fridge—if properly handled and with no contamination. As always, if you see, smell, or feel that something is wrong, check on the jar, and use your judgment if it's still good to eat. In time, you'll see that jars are not just for pickles.

# 4.1 Camping!

Sure, mason jars might be a bit heavy to lug around, but they are secure and sealed, so you will not be spilling your food around. Aside from ready-to-eat meals, you can also have some ready-to-cook meals wherein you will just have to add some water and warm it up by the campfire. Since the jars are sealed, you also won't be attracting much of the wildlife around you.

When assembling your meals for camping, you have to consider what you have to work with to finely tune your jarred meal game.

• No-cook or pre-cooked meals are always a good thing to have during your long treks or hikes.

• However, part of the joy of camping is sitting around the fire and having a meal. Like Samwise Gamgee, it's smart to bring a good skillet, a bit of oil, and maybe a small box of fine salt on your journey. This also allows you to have a nice warm meal when you want and need it.

• Aside from stir-frying or sauteing in a skillet, another viable way of warming your food is with a water bath using your pot. This option is only possible if you are camping in an area with cottages. You can also brew some hot coffee as you warm your meals. When doing this, however, you may need a towel to hold the warm jars. Do not put cold jars into hot water or hot jars in cold water, as it can cause the jars to crack and break. You should also open the jars, or at least loosen up the lid, so that the steam can escape.

• Not all meals are served hot. If you want a chilled meal, you can leave your mason jars outside the tent if the season permits. They're sealed so they won't attract wildlife. Another option is partially submerging them in a stream or lake overnight when the temperature drops to cool your food.

• Aside from carrying your meals, jars are quite useful in the great outdoors. They can carry your matches, and you can also use them for candles or lanterns, making sure that you don't accidentally start a forest fire.

## 4.1.1 Quinoa Salad

One of the most basic yet great meals in a jar. Quinoa is a great source of fiber and carbohydrates to keep you going, while the addition of cheese gives you lean proteins

22

to keep your antibodies up and your blood flowing.

Ingredients:

- 2 cups uncooked quinoa

- 1 whole broccoli

- 1 cup feta cheese

- 1 cup corn kernels

- 1 cup carrot, finely diced

- 1 tbsp. canola oil

- 1 tsp. ground sumac

- Salt and pepper to taste

Directions:

1. Cut off the florets of your broccoli, but do not throw the stalk away. Split the stalk lengthwise, so you can see what you are working with. Slice off the fibrous skin, and dice the core just like the carrots. Set these aside.

2. Pour the quinoa in a strainer set on top of a bowl. Give that a quick rinse under tap water, and let it drain dry. Set a pot over medium heat, and pour in 4 cups of water. Add the quinoa and the diced broccoli stalks.

3. Mix everything up, bring it to a boil, and then lower the heat to maintain a bare simmer. After 10 minutes into cooking time, drop in the corn kernels, carrot, and broccoli florets to steam for 5 minutes.

4. Once everything is cooked, give it a taste, and then add the sumac, salt, and pepper. Mix everything up and let it cool completely. Transfer into your jars and top with canola oil and feta cheese.

5. During camping, simply sauté in a hot pan to heat everything up, and enjoy straight out of the pan!

## 4.1.2 Chickpea Salad

This is a great salad for when you are on the go. Chickpea is rich in fiber and protein, which regulates your digestion and insulin levels—and that's just for the main ingredient. This recipe is packed with more healthy stuff. This recipe tastes good and is good for you!

Ingredients:

- 16 oz. canned chickpeas, rinsed and drained to get rid of the slime (use the chickpea liquid as a substitute for egg white in cocktails)

- 1 cup tomatoes, seeded and diced; use any variety that you like

- ½ cup cucumber, seeded and diced

- ½ cup bell pepper, seeded and diced; use any color you like

- 1 medium red onion, finely chopped

- ¼ cup basil, loosely packed, cut into ribbons

- 2 tbsp. fresh dill, finely chopped

- 1 tbsp. red wine vinegar

- 2 tbsp. good quality olive oil

- Salt and pepper to taste

Directions:

1. Drain your chickpeas and give them a good rinse. Just be careful not to crush them when rinsing. Transfer them into a bowl.

2. Cut your tomato in half and scoop out the seeds, as these will make your salad too watery. As for the cucumber, some people don't like to keep the peel on, while others don't mind. Just scoop out the seeds and chop them up. Chop up your bell pepper and onion as well.

3. Roll up your basil like a cigar, and cut them finely crosswise to make a chiffonade. As for the dill, they are already fine, so you can just run the knife through them. Transfer everything into the bowl with the chickpeas.

4. In a separate small bowl, mix the red wine and olive oil, and whisk them to get a slight emulsion. Give it a taste and season with salt and pepper. Whisk them to dissolve the salt.

5. Drizzle the vinaigrette all over the vegetables, and toss to coat. Distribute among your jars and close them up. Give it a good shake before consuming to make sure the vinaigrette does not pool at the bottom.

# 4.1.3 Jarred Omelet Mix

Part of the fun when camping is cooking around a campfire. Part of the unpleasantness of camping is cleaning up after yourself. So, instead of preparing your meals in the middle of the wilderness, why not prepare everything in the comfort and convenience of your kitchen? Omelets are great all-around meals, not just for breakfast but for lunch, dinner, and snacks too. Just pair them with different drinks depending on the time. Omelets are also good for fridge raiding and getting rid of leftovers.

Ingredients:

- Eggs, allot 2 eggs for each pint-sized jar

- Protein of your choice, you can have ham, sausages, bacon bits, or leftover roast chicken

- Vegetable of your choice, like peppers, onions, and herbs

- Cheese

- Salt and pepper to taste

Directions:

1. First, spray the inside of the jar and under the lid with non-stick spray. You can also use a bit of oil, close it up, and give it a good shake to coat the inside.

2. If you are using raw protein, cut them into small uniform pieces, and sauté them in a skillet with a bit of oil until cooked. If you are using cooked items, then proceed to assembly. Vegetables can be raw or cooked, depending on what you have. Just make sure to cut them into uniform sizes so that they can cook or at least heat up at the same time

3. Distribute the fillings among your jars, crack the eggs in, and add the seasoning. If you want something like a hash, you may add more fillings than eggs, and if you want an omelet or frittata style, then lessen the fillings.

4. Close the jar and give it a good shake to distribute the seasoning and scramble the eggs. Store in the fridge before you go on your camping trip.

5. To cook, set an oiled skillet on your fire. Shake the jar to remix everything inside before pouring into a hot

skillet. Alternatively, you can place the jars in a pot and pour enough water to fill halfway up the jars. Set it over or near the fire, and let it simmer until you get your preferred egg doneness. I prefer the water bath method since it makes some really fluffy eggs.

## 4.1.4 Seafood Fried Rice

You might think that it's a joke to have fried rice for a camping meal, but it's a good portable dish that you can just heat up on a really hot skillet or wok. Just don't forget that small container of oil, and don't confuse that with drinking water.

Ingredients:

- 2 cups uncooked rice; you can use white or brown

- ½ cup frozen shrimp, thawed and deveined

- ½ cup lump crab meat

- ½ large onion, finely chopped

- ½ cup frozen peas

- ¼ cup pineapple juice

- 2 tbsp. chives, finely chopped

- 1 tbsp. Old Bay seasoning, just because it's great

- 1 tbsp. fresh thyme

- Salt and pepper to taste

Directions:

1. About 2 to 3 days before your camping trip, cook the rice. Do this by rinsing the rice under cold water 2 to 3 times until the water runs clear. Transfer it to your rice cooker or pot with 3 to 4 cups of water, depending on the type of rice you are using. Gently simmer it for 15 minutes. You can actually cook a bigger batch than the 2 cups I've specified and eat the rest while they are freshly cooked.

2. For the fried rice, lay it even on an oiled baking dish or tray, and stash it in the fridge overnight.

3. The following day, take out the rice from the fridge. Set a skillet or wok over low flame; add a bit of oil and

about half a cup of finely chopped onion. Sprinkle a bit of salt to draw out the moisture. Cook until the onion has been browned and caramelized.

4. Increase the heat to medium, and pour in the pineapple juice and old bay seasoning. Let the pineapple juice reduce by about half.

5. Add the rice, and stir everything well until fully coated. Take it off the heat. In a large bowl, dump in the rice mixture, and add the shrimp, crab, peas, chives, thyme, salt, and pepper. You can add more Old Bay seasoning if you like. Mix everything well, and set it aside.

6. Spray the inside of the jar and under the lid with non-stick spray. You can also pour a bit of oil, close it up, give it a good shake to coat the inside, and then pour the oil that didn't stick into a different jar and repeat.

7. Distribute the partially cooked fried rice among the jars, and seal them tight. When reheating, simply dump the contents of a jar on a hot oiled pan, and cook until the seafood develops some color.

# 4.1.5 Frito Pie in a Jar

Admittedly, it's a bit of a cheat to incorporate some junk food here, but hey—you're hiking and wandering about in the wilderness, so you can definitely handle a bit more calories. Also, this method makes this meal cheap yet nutritious and filling. An all-around winner! I do have another chili recipe in the canning section of this book, so this will be a quick chili-and-beans version.

Ingredients:

- 1 lb. ground beef

- 16 oz. canned pinto beans drained and rinsed

- 1 cup salsa

- 1 cup beef broth

- 1 cup chili pepper, seeded and sliced; you may use bell peppers, poblanos, or even jalapenos

- 3 cloves of garlic, peeled and finely grated

- 1 tbsp. chili powder

- 2 tsp. ground cumin

- Grated cheddar cheese

- Salt and pepper to taste

Directions:

1. Set a pot over medium heat, and add a bit of oil. Once hot, sauté the ground beef until browned. Add the chili pepper, garlic, chili powder, and cumin. Sauté until fragrant and the garlic is cooked.

2. Deglaze the pot with the salsa and broth, scraping the bottom to loosen up any stuck bits. Bring this to a boil, and then lower the heat to maintain a bare simmer. Cook for about 30 minutes. Give it a taste and season accordingly.

3. Once cooked, take the chili off the heat and let it cool down to room temperature. To assemble, here you have some options. If you want your Fritos crispy, you can fill up the jar with chili and cheese and pour in the bag of Fritos—the usual way. However, if you are like me and want your Fritos a little bit soggy from the chili, you can fill the jars only halfway with the chili, add a good layer of

cheese, and fill the rest with Fritos.

4. To reheat, simply pour the contents in a pot and gently heat in the camp fire. Alternatively, you can place the jar in the pot half-filled with water and gently heat it up. Just be careful with the hot jar when eating. You also have the option of swapping out the Fritos with corn bread or rice.

## 4.1.6 Next-Level Keto Egg Salad

Egg salads get a bad rap because they're basically fat on fat, plus a load of carbs when you eat them as a sandwich. However, they do taste good, so why don't we tweak it a bit and make it a complete meal? Make calories work for you with just the right amount of energy for the day. You can also think of this recipe as an improved keto egg salad.

Ingredients:

• 4 large hard-boiled eggs

• 1 rotisserie chicken breast or leftover roast chicken breast, boneless with the skin on or off

- ¼ cup Greek yogurt, plain and unsweetened

- ¼ cup mayonnaise, low-fat if you like

- 1 tbsp. Dijon mustard

- 1 tsp. smoked paprika

- 1 cup arugula, roughly chopped

- 1 cup kale leaves, finely chopped

- ¼ cup chives, finely chopped

- Salt and pepper to taste

Directions:

1. Boil your eggs in water with a bit of white vinegar added for 8 minutes, then shock them in ice cold water. When they are cool enough to handle, peel the eggs. Set these aside.

2. Shred the chicken breast with forks, and transfer them into a bowl. Chop up the eggs into large chunks since they will break down more during mixing, and add to the bowl. Then, pour in the yogurt, mayonnaise,

mustard, paprika, arugula, kale, and chives.

3. Mix everything up and give it a taste. Season accordingly before transferring into jars. You can enjoy it slightly chilled or at room temperature. You can have it as a side dish, but it really works as your main meal.

## 4.1.7 Individual Shepherd's Pie

Pasta dishes are easy to prepare and easy to eat as well. I mean, who doesn't like pasta? A vegetarian pesto is healthy, nutritious, and filling. You can add some meat if you want or even pair it with some bread.

Ingredients:

- 2 cups homemade or store-bought mashed potato; use your favorite brand or recipe

- 1 lb. ground beef

- 2 cups beef broth

- 1 medium carrot, diced

- 2 garlic cloves, finely grated

- 1 tbsp. tomato paste

- 1 tbsp. Worcestershire sauce

- 1 tbsp. ground fennel seeds

- 2 bay leaves

- Salt and pepper to taste

Directions:

1. Set a pot over medium heat, and add a bit of oil. Once hot, sauté the ground beef until browned. Add the carrot and garlic. Sauté until fragrant and the garlic is cooked.

2. Add the tomato paste and fennel seeds, let it sauté for a few seconds, and then deglaze everything with the broth. Give it a good mix, drop the bay leaves, and let it simmer for about 30 minutes.

3. Take the stew off the heat and add the Worcestershire sauce to keep things fresh, then round out the flavors. Let the stew cool down a bit. Distribute it among your jars, leaving about 2 inches of head space for

the mashed potato. Seal it tight.

4. To heat up, just place them in a water bath—lids off, of course—and enjoy.

## 4.1.8 Seafood Boil

We are familiar with these crustacean boils in the South, which usually accompany large events. Why not also enjoy them in the comfort of your camp? You can partially boil everything at home and just add hot water to reheat.

Ingredients:

• 2 lbs. crustaceans of your choice; you may use crawfish, crabs, lobster, shrimp, or a mix

• 2 Andouille sausages, cut into bite-sized pieces

• 2 cups corn kernels or baby corn

• ½ lbs. baby red potatoes, washed and cut into halves or quarters depending on the size

• 3 garlic cloves, peeled and lightly crushed

- 2 tbsp. Old Bay seasoning.

- 1 tbsp. lemon juice

- Salt and pepper to taste

Directions:

1. Set a pot over medium heat and fill it a quarter of the way up with water. Bring the water to a boil before adding the sausage and potatoes. Form to a layer, and then add the crustaceans so they can just steam for about 15 minutes, covered.

2. For the last 3 minutes of cooking time, add the corn kernels if you are using fresh raw kernels. Take it off the heat and drain everything, saving the broth for future recipes. Distribute the potatoes and sausages among your jars. If you are using canned corn kernels, distribute them straight into the jars.

3. For the crustaceans, remove the shells, taking out as much of the meat and the good stuff as you can. Distribute these among your jars, and get rid of the shells. This also gives you space for more food in your jars. Devein the shrimp and lobsters, of course.

4. Sprinkle some Old Bay lemon juice, salt, and pepper into each jar before sealing shut. To reheat, carefully pour warm water into each jar. When the jars are cold, place them in a pot with water and slowly warm them on the fire before pouring hot water inside.

## 4.1.9 Tuna Salad Dip

Tuna salad sandwiches are nice, but they don't leave you with many options. These tuna salad dips give you more options and are less messy to lug around. You can have them with bread, toast, crackers, celery stalks, or with just a spoon. You can even top them with the broken chips in your bag.

Ingredients:

- 10 oz. or 2 cans tuna in water or oil

- 1 medium cucumber, seeded and diced

- 1 small red onion, finely diced

- ½ cup mayonnaise

- 2 tbsp. fresh parsley

- 1 tbsp. mustard

- Salt and pepper to taste

Directions:

1. Drain your tuna, and transfer them into a large bowl. Split the cucumber in half lengthwise, and use a spoon to scoop out the seeds and membrane in the middle. If you keep this in, it will turn your dip watery later, so better remove them. Chop them up into small dice. Chop up your onion and parsley as well, and dump them into the bowl.

2. Add the mayonnaise and mustard and mix. Give it a taste and season accordingly. You can also add a bit more mayonnaise if you want it creamier and more spreadable. Distribute among your jars, and wipe off the rim before sealing. If you have used tuna in oil, you may pour the oil on top of the dip and stash it in the fridge to solidify, forming a barrier and preventing oxidation.

## 4.1.10 Granola Jars

You can't go out on a camping trip without bringing granola. It's a handy snack, but it turns into a meal for tough trails. It gives you protein, fiber, and sugar to keep you going.

Ingredients:

- 3 cups rolled oats

- 1 cup slivered almonds

- 1 cup chopped walnuts

- ½ cup pistachios, shelled and chopped

- ¼ cup raisins

- ¼ cup dried cranberries

- ¼ cup dried apricots, finely chopped

- 1/3 cup brown sugar

- 1/3 cup honey

- 2 tbsp. coconut oil

- Pinch of salt

Directions:

1. Preheat your oven to 250°F. Mix the oats, almonds, walnuts, pistachios, brown sugar, and salt in a large bowl to distribute it evenly. Mix the oil and honey in a bowl to get a good emulsion, and pour it in the granola mixture.

2. Quickly mix everything to coat each piece, and spread them on a lightly oiled baking sheet. Make sure they occupy a single thin layer. Bake in the oven for 1 hour and 15 minutes, stirring every 15 to 20 minutes.

3. Once everything is crunchy and the honey mixture is absorbed, let it completely cool to room temperature.

4. Transfer the baked granola into a bowl, and mix in the dried fruits. Mix everything well and distribute among your jars. Add an oxygen absorber before sealing it up.

## 4.2 The Office

Making jarred meals for you to bring to the office is similar to camping - but with more convenience.

- You have a limited option for reheating food in the

office, which is mainly the microwave. Luckily, mason jars are microwave-safe - just remove the metal lid and screw bands. Also, don't put frozen or chilled mason jars in the microwave to keep them from cracking.

• Be careful when handling mason jars from the microwave since they can become really hot, especially when zapped for a long time.

• On the other side of the spectrum, mason jars are reliably refrigerator-safe, so they are perfect for chilled meals. For freezing, make sure to check with your particular brand of jars if they can handle the freezer. Don't put too much liquid in since the ice can burst them open.

• Unlike with camping, you don't have much margin in the way of time in the office, so ready-to-eat or ready-to-warm meals are best.

• You also have limited space in the office, particularly if you eat at your table, so eating straight from the jar is a good option. Besides, I don't like my co-workers to see me spreading pate on toast and sprinkling herbs in the office.

• Another benefit of eating straight from the jar is the

time saved in cleaning. Lunch boxes have different parts which you have to clean. With a jar, you just have to clean the jar and a fork or spoon.

## 4.2.1 Leftover BBQ in a Jar

Have some leftover food from your BBQ party over the weekend? Then why not extend it through your week? Have the flavors of summer even when you are at the office with this recipe.

Ingredients:

- 2 lbs. pulled pork, grilled chicken, or beef brisket

- 2 cups baked beans

- 2 cups mashed potatoes

- BBQ sauce, your favorite brand, to taste

Directions:

1. Clean your jars and line them up. If you are using grilled chicken or brisket, shred them up or cut them into

smaller pieces. Remove any bones, cartilage, or gristle.

2. Simply layer your leftovers for a complete meal. Start off with the beans, then a good layer of mashed potato, and finally, the meat. Pour on the BBQ on top, depending on how much you like it.

3. To reheat, simply stick it in the microwave on high for a minute or 2. A good trick is to have a mug or cup half filled with water in the microwave to keep things moist and to heat it up evenly.

## 4.2.2 Roasted Pepper Soup

I like having soup at the office since I just warm it up and drink it straight from the jar like coffee. It saves me time on the clean-up, and I can get back to working on those deadlines.

Ingredients:

- 1 lb. red bell peppers

- 4 cups chicken or vegetable broth

- 1 large white onion, roughly chopped

• Salt and pepper to taste

Directions:

1. Fire up your stove or grill on high, and burn the peppers directly over the flame. Work in batches if you are just using the stove, and transfer the blackened pepper into a bowl covered with the plate.

2. Let the peppers steam in the bowl for about 10 minutes or until they are cool enough to the touch. They should be easy enough to peel now. Remove the steam and seeds, and transfer the peeled peppers to the plate. It's fine if there are some specks of the charred skin left - they will add a smoky flavor.

3. Set a pot over medium heat and add a bit of oil. Once hot, sauté the onions until translucent. Add the peppers and continue to cook for about 5 minutes to caramelize.

4. Deglaze the pot with the broth and bring it to a boil. Lower the heat to maintain a bare simmer for about 15 minutes, uncovered. After cooking time, use a stick blender and process everything until smooth. You may also use your bar blender, working in batches.

5. Once pureed, let it cool down to room temperature before distributing among your jars.

### 4.2.3 Cobb Salad

Cobb salads are healthy and great-tasting. The addition of bacon and boiled eggs gives it a nice protein and fat boost to keep you going through the day.

Ingredients:

- 4 hard-boiled egg, peeled cut in halves

- 1 lb. raw bacon

- 2 cups rotisserie or roast chicken breast, boneless and cut into bite-sized pieces

- 4 cups Romaine lettuce, chopped

- 8 cherry tomatoes, quartered

- ½ cup blue cheese crumbled

- ¼ cup olive oil

- 2 tbsp. red wine vinegar

- 1 tbsp. lemon juice

- 1 tbsp. Worcestershire sauce

- Salt and pepper to taste

Directions:

1. Mix the olive oil, red wine vinegar, lemon juice, Worcestershire sauce, salt, and pepper in a small jar. Close it up and give it a good shake. Keep the vinaigrette in the fridge, and just pour some before you leave for work.

2. Fry up the bacon to your desired crispness, and break them up into bite-sized pieces. Cut the eggs in half, just so that the vinaigrette can seep into the tasty yolk. Shred the chicken with a fork or chop it up, depending on your preference.

3. Chop up the lettuce and cut the tomatoes into 4 wedges each.

4. Get 4 16 oz.-mason jars. Stuff each one with an egg, bacon, chicken, lettuce, 2 tomatoes, and blue cheese. Close them up and store in the fridge. Just shake up the jar

before you eat to distribute the vinaigrette in case it pools at the bottom.

## 4.2.4 Jarred Chicken Noodle Soup

Cup noodles are the cornerstone meal of any college student or penny-pincher out there. I mean, who can blame them? They're cheap, tasty, and filling - but not quite healthy. So, why not pump it up a bit and make a healthy jarred noodle to snack on in the office?

Ingredients:

- 2 cups parboiled noodles

- 2 cups cooked chicken breast, boneless, shredded

- 1 large carrot, finely chopped

- 1 celery stalk, finely chopped

- 1 chicken bouillon cube

- 2 tbsp. olive oil

- 2 tbsp. dried thyme

- Salt and pepper to taste

Directions:

1. In a small bowl, mix the bouillon cube and the 2 tablespoons of olive oil until you form a paste. Distribute that paste into 4 16 oz.-jars.

2. Layer on the chicken, noodles, carrot, and celery. Sprinkle on some dried thyme. Seal the jars up and store them in the fridge if you are not bringing them to work.

3. To reheat, simply pour in hot water and wait for a minute or 2 to completely warm everything up.

## 4.2.5 Sesame Noodles

Another quick noodle dish, but this time, it's good to eat whether warm or chilled. It may sound fancy, but you can actually make it with peanut butter. Plus, this is a good recipe to add value to ordinary packaged instant noodles.

Ingredients:

- 4 packs instant noodles, I normally don't use the

flavor packs, but you may save that for some quick soups or for sprinkling over some eggs

- 4 hard-boiled eggs, you can skip this if you want it to be vegetarian

- ½ cup scallion, finely chopped

- 1 cup smooth peanut butter, just any regular grocery brand will do

- 1 tbsp soy sauce

- 1 tbsp. black vinegar

- ½ tbsp sesame oil

- 1 tbsp. chili oil, more or less if you like

- Sugar to taste

Directions:

1. In a large bowl, mix the peanut butter, soy sauce, vinegar, sesame oil, chili oil, and sugar. It's quite difficult to mix since the peanut butter is thick, but don't worry about it too much. Just do what you can.

2. Cook the noodles in boiling water as instructed in the package. As the noodles cook, take some of the boiling water and add it to the peanut butter mixture to loosen it up and so that you can mix it up properly.

3. Take out the noodles from the water and immediately transfer them into the bowl with the peanut butter sauce. Toss it well to coat every strand of noodle, and portion them out into your jars.

4. Top with sliced boiled eggs and scallions. You can zap it in the microwave for a few seconds before consuming or eat it straight from the fridge.

## 4.2.6 Taco Jar

Why go through the trouble of standing in line in a fast food chain to get a taco bowl when you can easily make it at home? Heat it up in the microwave, and start munching away on the taco goodness.

Ingredients:

- 1 lb. ground beef

- 1 cup lettuce, chopped

- 1 medium white onion, finely chopped

- 1 cup salsa

- ½ cup sharp cheddar grated

- 1 tbsp. ground cumin

- 1 tbsp. chili powder

- Tortilla chips, crushed

- Salt and pepper to taste

Directions:

1. Place the ground beef in a bowl, and sprinkle on the ground cumin, chili powder, salt and pepper. Set a skillet over medium heat and add a bit of oil. Once hot, sauté the seasoned beef until fully cooked. Drain off the excess oil, and let it cool down to room temperature.

2. As the beef cools down, clean your jars, and chop up your vegetables. First, place a thick layer of beef. Then spoon in some salsa, cheese, onion, and lettuce. Top up each jar with some tortilla chips.

3. Store the jars in the fridge until you need to take one to work. To reheat, just open it up and then zap in the microwave for a few seconds to warm up the salsa and meat.

## 4.2.7 Energy Boost Oatmeal

This recipe gives you your needed fiber, carbs, and protein, with a little bit of sugar and caffeine to energize you through your workday.

Ingredients:

- 2 cups rolled oats

- 2 cups milk

- 1 cup plain yogurt

- ½ cup slivered almonds

- ¼ cup honey

- ¼ cup peanut butter

- 1 tbsp. granulated coffee

- Pinch of salt

- Frozen fruits, you can use banana slices or berries

Directions:

1. Pour the milk, yogurt, honey, and peanut butter in a bowl, and mix them well until the honey and peanut butter are fully integrated.

2. Once the liquids are well mixed, add the oats, almonds, coffee and salt. Mix them well and transfer into jars. Store in the fridge. Before you leave for work, top each jar with frozen fruits, and then seal shut.

# 4.3 Quick Home Meals

You may have all the arsenal to make you and your family a meal at home, but sometimes, you might just be short on time and patience.

• You have the option of making ready-to-cook jarred meals at home. You will still need to cook them, but you will cut down on a large chunk of preparation time.

• Cooking jarred meals at home gives you the convenience of having warm and delicious meals quicker.

• Ready-to-cook meals also last longer in storage than

ready-to-eat or ready-to-heat meals, taking advantage of the availability of storage compartments in your home.

• Guests sometimes arrive unexpectedly, or sometimes you have cravings, so having jarred meals is pretty handy at home. It allows you to accommodate everyone with less stress.

## 4.3.1 Jarred Burrito

This jarred burrito recipe is quite versatile, as you can enjoy it in several ways. You can heat it up in a skillet and transfer it into a bowl. You can heat it up and wrap it in some warm tortilla. If you really can't be bothered, you can just open up the jar and stash in the microwave for a minute.

Ingredients:

• 2 cups uncooked rice

• 4 cups beef or pork broth

• ½ lb. ground beef

• ½ lb. ground pork

- 15 oz. of pinto beans, rinsed and drained

- 1 cup chili peppers, seeded and finely chopped, your choice of variety

- 1 large red onion, finely chopped

- ½ cup salsa

- 1 tbsp. chili powder

- 1 tbsp. ground cumin

- Sharp cheddar cheese, grated

- Salt and pepper to taste

Directions:

1. Set a wide pot over medium heat, and add a bit of oil. Once hot, sauté the onion and peppers until the onions are translucent. Then add the beef and a pinch of salt, and continue to sauté until the beef is fully cooked.

2. Drain off excess oil, only keeping about a tablespoon in the pot. Add the rice, chili powder, and cumin, and mix them until the spices become really fragrant. Add the

beans and salsa, and deglaze everything with the broth. Add a small pinch of salt and a lot of pepper. Mix everything up, making sure nothing sticks at the bottom.

3. Bring to a boil, and then lower the heat to maintain a bare simmer. Cover the pot, and let it cook for about 15 minutes or until the rice is tender. Once cooked, take it off the heat, and fluff it up to keep it from sticking at the bottom. Give it a taste, and season accordingly, if needed.

4. As the burrito rice cools down, rub a bit of oil into your jars or use a non-stick spray. Transfer the cooled-down rice into the jars and top it with some cheddar cheese. To reheat, simply transfer the contents of a jar into a non-stick pan or zap in your microwave, then you can eat it as is or wrapped in a tortilla.

## 4.3.2 Bibimbap in a Pop

This Korean rice dish hits all the notes. Not only is it flavorful and great, but it's also meant to make use of the leftover vegetables you have. It has some meat for protein and is loaded with vegetables, making it a relatively healthy dish. Now for this recipe, let's shake it up a bit. Instead of mixing in the rice, which takes up more space, we fill the jar up with only the toppings and the sauce.

You just have to mix it with some rice on the stove and enjoy.

Ingredients:

- 1 lb. ground beef

- 2 cups bean sprouts

- 1 cup spinach, tightly packed

- 1 cup shiitake mushrooms

- 1 large carrot, cut into matchsticks

- 1/2 cup gochujang

- ¼ cup. sesame oil

- ¼ cup. sugar

- ¼ cup. soy sauce

- 2 tbsp. rice wine vinegar

- 2 tbsp. garlic paste

- Sesame seeds

Directions:

1. Set a pot over medium heat and half fill it with water. Add a big pinch of salt, and bring it to a boil. Once on a rolling boil, add the bean sprouts and spinach and boil for 2 minutes. Set them aside to completely drain.

2. Mix the gochujang, sesame oil, sugar, soy sauce, rice wine vinegar, and garlic paste in a bowl. Mix until fully integrated, and set this aside.

3. Set a large skillet or wok over medium heat, and add a bit of oil. Add the ground beef and sauté until browned. Then add the carrots and mushrooms, and sauté until the carrots are slightly tender.

4. Add the sauce and the blanched vegetables, and mix until everything is coated. The consistency should be quite loose because of the excess sauce, but it's there to flavor the rice that you are going to mix with it.

5. Transfer 2 cups of the bibimbap mixture in each jar, and sprinkle on sesame seeds. Let it completely cool before screwing on the lid and stashing in the fridge. For

reheating and serving, heat up the contents of 1 jar in a large skillet with 3 to 4 cups of cooked rice. Mix in a raw egg before plating, and sprinkle with a lot of nori flakes.

## 4.3.3 Mapo Tofu

Let's move on to China with their really spicy yet appetizing dish, the mapo tofu. It's a stir-fried ground meat dish with lots of spice, plus the highly fragrant and flavorful Szechuan peppercorns, which add a numbing mouthfeel to the dish. The heat is somehow mitigated by the addition of a bit of sugar and the creaminess of silken tofu. It's great on its own, over rice or even noodles.

Ingredients:

- 1 lb. silken tofu, cut into inch cubes

- ½ lb. ground beef

- ½ lb. ground pork

- 2 cups pork broth

- 2-inch piece of ginger, finely grated

- 1 whole head of garlic, finely grated

- 2 tbsp. spicy bean sauce, like doubanjiang or gochujang, but you may also use black bean sauce or doenjang for less spice

- 1 tbsp. red chili flakes

- 1 tbsp. chili oil

- 1 tbsp. Szechuan peppercorn, finely ground

- 1 tbsp. sesame oil

- ¼ cup water

- 1 tbsp. cornstarch

- Sugar to taste

Directions:

1. Set a large skillet or wok over medium heat, and add a bit of oil. Once hot, sauté the ginger and garlic until fragrant. Then add the pork and beef, and sauté until fully cooked. Keep the meat moving to break it down into smaller pieces and to cook evenly.

2. Add the spicy bean sauce, chili flakes, chili oil, Szechuan peppercorn, and sesame oil. Keep on mixing so that the spices won't burn. Let this cook for about a minute before dousing everything with the broth. Scrape the bottom for any stuck bits, and mix thoroughly. Lower the heat to a simmer, and let this cook for about 5 minutes.

3. In the meantime, mix a quarter cup of water and a tablespoon of cornstarch in a small bowl. Also, have your cut tofu cubes ready.

4. Pour the cornstarch slurry into the wok and mix it well. Add the tofu and gently mix them in to keep their shape. Give this a taste, and add sugar to your liking. Let everything simmer for another 5 minutes before taking it off the heat to cool down.

5. Distribute it among your jars, and let it completely cool before stashing in the fridge. To reheat, simply place the jar at room temperature in the microwave.

## 4.3.4 Pasta and Meatballs

Kids and adults alike love pasta and meatballs. They are easily recognizable and have simple flavors that the kids like while bringing a nostalgic flair for the adults. It's ubiquitous and is perfect for a family meal.

Ingredients:

- 1 lb. pasta, spaghetti is the classic, but you can also have your children pick out their favorite shapes

- ¼ lb. ground beef

- ¼ lb. ground pork

- ¼ lb. ground lamb

- 12 oz jarred marinara sauce

- 1 whole egg

- 1 cup bread crumbs

- 2 tbsp. Italian seasoning

- 1 tbsp. garlic powder

- Salt and pepper to taste

Directions:

1. Place the meats in a bowl, and add in the bread crumbs, a tablespoon of the Italian seasoning, and half a tablespoon of the garlic powder. Add a pinch of salt and pepper and crack the egg over the top. Make your kids wear some gloves and allow them to mix everything up. Also, teach them to form the meat mixture into small bite-sized balls. As they do that, preheat your oven to 375°F.

2. Have your kids place the meatballs in a lightly oiled baking sheet or tray. Form them into a single layer, and bake in the oven for about 15 minutes or until golden brown and delicious. Let it cool completely to room temperature when done.

3. Set 2 pots over medium heat. In one pot, add a bit of oil, and pour in the marinara sauce with the remaining Italian seasoning and garlic powder. Let this simmer for about 10 minutes. Give it a taste and season accordingly.

4. In the other pot, fill it halfway with water and add a big pinch of salt. Boil the pasta until it's tender to the touch but still with a bit of a crunch inside. Drain the pasta and let it cool completely.

5. To assemble, mix the pasta, meatballs, and the sauce into a bowl. Carefully mix them to coat, and then transfer

into your jars. Wipe off any smudge on the rim, close the lid, and stash in the fridge. To reheat, simply empty the jar into a pan and heat on the stove. Sprinkle on some parmesan cheese before enjoying.

## 4.3.5 Shrimp and Oats

This is a play on the classic Southern shrimp and grits, a staple breakfast item made easier by mixing them with overnight oats. Just heat them up on a stove and enjoy!

Ingredients:

- ½ lb. shrimp tails, deveined and shell removed

- 6 strips of bacon, cut into bite-sized pieces

- 3 cups oats

- 4 cups milk

- 2 cups heavy cream

- 2 cups sharp cheddar cheese, shredded

- 1 tbsp. lemon juice

- 1 tsp. garlic powder

- 1 tsp. dried thyme

- 1 tsp. black pepper

Directions:

1. Set a skillet over medium heat, and cook the bacon to your desired doneness. Drain the bacon, but return a tablespoon of the bacon grease into the skillet. Sauté the shrimp in the bacon grease, and sprinkle on the lemon juice, garlic powder, thyme, and black pepper. Take it off the heat, and let it cool to room temperature.

2. As the shrimp cools, mix the oats, milk, cream, and cheese in a bowl. Transfer into jars, and top with the shrimp mixture. Stash in the fridge. To reheat, simply pour the contents of a jar in a buttered hot skillet.

## 4.3.6 Vegetarian Pesto Pasta

Pasta dishes are easy to prepare and easy to eat as well. I mean, who doesn't like pasta? A vegetarian pesto is healthy, nutritious, and filling. You can add some meat if you want or even pair it with some bread.

Ingredients:

- 2 cups dried fusilli, orecchiette, or rotini, they hold on to the sauce really well, and they are easy to stuff into the jar

- 1 cup basil leaves, packed

- 1 cup fresh spinach leaves, packed

- ¼ cup pine nuts

- 3 cloves of garlic, peeled

- 4 to 6 cherry tomatoes, quartered

- Olive oil

- Salt and pepper to taste

Directions:

1. Dump the basil, spinach, pine nuts, and garlic into your food processor. Process them while slowly drizzling some olive oil. Add enough oil to get the right consistency. It should be quite thick without forming a paste. Give it a taste and season accordingly.

2. Set a pot over medium heat and half-fill it with water. Bring to a boil, and add a bit of salt. Once boiling, add your pasta of choice. Cook until just before the point of al dente. They will cook more when reheated.

3. Transfer the parboiled pasta into a bowl, and pour the pesto sauce all over. Toss to coat and transfer into the jars. Top with some tomatoes, and seal.

4. To reheat, just toss the contents of the jar in a hot skillet, and enjoy!

## 4.3.7 California Maki in a Jar

I wanted to put sushi here, but fresh fish doesn't last that long in the fridge with other ingredients. Instead, we are going to use vegetables and lump crab meat. You can also put in some imitation crab sticks if you like. Hey, it may not be real, but it tastes good when well-made.

Ingredients:

- 2 cups uncooked sushi rice

- 2 tbsp. rice wine vinegar

- 2 tbsp. sugar

- 1 tsp. salt

- 1 cup lump crab meat or imitation crab sticks, finely chopped

- ½ cup cucumber, thinly sliced into discs or half-discs

- ½ cup carrot, thinly sliced into discs

- Nori flakes

Directions:

1. Use a kitchen mandolin to thinly slice the cucumber and carrot. Set these aside. Cook the rice according to the package.

2. As the rice cooks, dissolve the salt and sugar in the rice wine vinegar. Once the rice is cooked, transfer it into a bowl. Drizzle on the vinegar mixture, and gently fold it in to distribute. Be careful not to overwork the rice because it can get mushy and gummy. Just fold it to integrate the sauce. Let this cool to room temperature.

3. Have your jars ready, and sprinkle a bit of nori at the bottom. Layer on the rice, crab, cucumber, and finally, the carrot. Repeat this sequence until you reach the top, closing it off with a final layer of nori. Close the lid, and stash in the fridge. You can eat it chilled, straight from the fridge, or let it heat up to room temperature.

## 4.3.8 Individual Chicken Pot Pies

Chicken pot pies are usually a weekend meal, but you can have them in the middle of the week with this recipe. This recipe prepares the filling, which you simply need to place on a crust. There's even a shortcut for that - this recipe is for chicken pot pie that you can store in the fridge, and it'll last for about a week. If you want something that lasts longer, check out the canned chicken pot pie filling recipe in this book.

Ingredients:

• 3 cups cooked chicken breast or leftover rotisserie chicken breast, shredded

• 2 cups chicken broth

• 1 cup frozen peas

- 1 large carrot, finely diced

- 1 large onion, finely chopped

- ½ cup heavy cream

- ¼ cup butter

- ¼ cup flour

- Salt and pepper to taste

Directions:

1. Set a pot or deep skillet over medium heat, and melt the butter. Add the onion and carrots, and cook until the onion is translucent. Add the flour, salt, and pepper, then mix it around. There should not be any flecks of uncooked flour.

2. Slowly drizzle in the broth and cream, making sure that the flour mixture fully dissolves before pouring all the broth in. Add the peas and chicken to heat through, and let it simmer until you have a thick stew. Give it a taste and adjust the seasoning if needed.

3. Take the filling off the heat and let it cool to room temperature. Distribute it among your jars. Seal and store in the fridge.

4. To reheat, get some store-bought pie dough or puff pastry and cut out some discs of dough that can fit inside the mason jar. Bake the discs, and then place on top of the microwaved jar of chicken pot pie filling. If you are lazy like me or in a hurry, you can also pour the warmed chicken pot pie filling over some hot buttered biscuits or just top with some crackers.

## 4.4 The Jarring Kids

Cooking with kids should not be the stressful and messy activity that we envision it to be. Here are some pointers when making meals in jars with kids.

• Food preparation and cooking are vital life skills. Take this opportunity to show kids how to prepare their own food in a proper and sanitary manner. Teach them the value of a schedule so you can prepare your daily meals over the weekend, giving you more time for the rest of the week.

- Teach your kids about nutrition and how to balance their meals. Show them what foods are good for their health and how to have them in a tasty manner.

- Give them the freedom to exercise their creativity when choosing recipes and flavors. Couple this with nutrition, and they will be great home cooks in no time.

## 4.4.1 Freestyle Quiche

You and your kids may find frittata or omelets quite boring, so why not go a step further and upgrade your shell game? Quiche is a nice savory custard that is a leftover magnet. As long as you have the custard base established, you may put anything you like in it, or better yet, have your kids pick out what they like.

Ingredients:

- 4 large eggs

- 1 cup heavy cream

- ½ cup milk

- 1 ½ cup cheese, shredded; you may choose any you

like

- 1 cup ham, chopped into bite-sized pieces

- ½ cup mushroom

- ½ cup frozen peas

- 1 tbsp. dried basil

- 1 tsp. nutmeg

- Salt and pepper to taste

Directions:

1. Coat the inside of your jar with non-stick spray, oil, or butter. Set these aside.

2. Set a pan over medium heat, add a bit of oil, and cook the ham and mushrooms. Drain any excess oil, and let them cool to room temperature.

3. In a large bowl, add the eggs, cream, milk, cheese, peas, basil, nutmeg, and the cooked ham and mushrooms. Add a good pinch of salt and pepper, and mix everything up until fully integrated.

4. Ladle the custard into the jars, and wipe off any smudge on the rim. Place them in your microwave, and zap for a minute. The mixture should still be loose at this point, so give each jar a gentle mix to suspend everything and cook for another 30 seconds until the surface is solidified but still jiggly. They will cook more as they cool down. I suggest leaving them in the microwave with the door open after cooking time to let it cool down.

5. Alternatively, you can also cover the mouths of the jars with some cling wrap and steam them. Mix halfway through by lifting the plastic wraps a bit, stirring with a spoon or small spatula, and then covering again. The plastic wraps prevent the condensate from settling on the quiche's surface and creating a pool of water.

6. Once cooked, let it completely cool to room temperature before sealing with the lid and storing in the fridge. To reheat, just zap it again for a few seconds in the microwave, but they are also good to be enjoyed chilled.

## 4.4.2 Mac and Cheese

Ahhh, mac and cheese - something that's sought after by kids and people who have the munchies alike. You can't blame them, really. Mac and cheese is a comforting classic that should always be ready on hand or in the fridge in our case.

Ingredients:

- ½ lb., elbow macaroni pasta

- 1 cup frozen spinach

- 1 cup sharp cheddar cheese, shredded

- 1 cup milk

- 2 tbsp. butter

- 2 eggs

- 1 tsp. smoked paprika

- Salt and pepper to taste

Directions:

1. Whisk together the milk, eggs, salt, and pepper in a bowl. Set this aside.

2. Cook the macaroni and frozen spinach in boiling

salted water just until barely al dente, about 3 to 6 minutes. Drain, and then return everything to the pot.

3. While the pasta and pot are still hot, add the butter and mix to coat each piece of the pasta and spinach.

4. Return the pot of pasta over low heat, and pour in the milk mixture and the cheese. Allow this to cook, stirring often until the cheese is melted and everything is creamy. Take it off the heat and let it cool to room temperature.

5. Transfer into jars and store in the fridge. To reheat, you can add a teaspoon of water and zap in the microwave for a minute, or you can warm it up on the stove.

## 4.4.3 Exciting Asian Noodles

While pasta and cheese is a classic combination, the palette of a child is quite fickle and can change at any moment. This Asian-inspired noodle dish is a fusion of Thai, Japanese, and Indonesian flavors that livens up the noodles and is a perfect change of pace from really rich dishes.

Ingredients:

- 1 lb. egg noodles

- 1 cup snap peas, chopped into bite-sized pieces

- 1 cup sweet corn kernels

- ½ cup cooked and chopped bacon

- 2 tbsp. sesame oil

- 2 tbsp. bacon fat

- 1 tbsp. lime juice

- 1 tbsp. soy sauce

- 1 tbsp. peanut butter

- Salt and pepper to taste

Directions:

1. Cook the noodles according to the package, and set them aside to drain and cool down. Get a bowl, and mix together the sesame oil, bacon fat, lime juice, soy sauce, and peanut butter. Give it a taste and adjust the seasoning if needed.

2. Divide the noodles among your jars, filling them more than halfway to the top. Layer on the corn kernels and snap peas, and drizzle on the sauce. When serving, you can eat it chilled or warmed up on a pan, but definitely serve it with some wonton chips on top.

## 4.4.4 Yogurt Parfait

Kids love sweet stuff - I think that's just a universal law. I've seen some kids demand desserts without eating anything else. To be honest, we can also admit that we have cravings at some point. In order to lessen this, why don't we make something sweet that can also provide necessary nutrients to the little ones?

Ingredients:

• 32 oz. plain yogurt

• 2 cups fresh or frozen apples, peeled, seeded, and diced

• 2 cups fresh or frozen peaches, peeled, pitted, and diced

• 1 cup raisins

- 1 cup granola

- 1 tbsp. butter

- 2 tsp. cinnamon

- Honey, to your liking

- Pinch of salt

Directions:

1. Set a skillet over medium heat and melt the butter. Dump in the apple, peach, and raisins. Add the cinnamon and sprinkle a little bit of salt. The fruits will release some liquid, so let it reduce by about half or until the mixture looks syrupy. If the mixture is still loose, you may pour in a slurry made with a tablespoon each of flour and water.

2. Give the fruit mixture a taste and add honey to adjust the sweetness. Keep in mind that this mixture will also sweeten the yogurt, so adjust the sweetness accordingly. Take it off the heat, and let it cool down and thicken.

3. To assemble, place a layer of the fruit mixture at the bottom of the jar and then a layer of yogurt. Continue layering until you are about an inch and a half to the top. Fill up the rest of the space with granola. Close the lids, and store in the fridge.

## 4.5 Healthy Meal in a Bottle

Aside from storage, placing meals in a jar is also a good method of portion control, making it easier to count your calories within a day.

• Measure the amount of food you are preparing, and measure them properly. You may have to use smaller jars like the 8 oz.-size for individual servings.

• Whenever it's time for a meal, simply reach for a jar, warm it up or cook it, and you know you are eating within your limits.

• Too much of a good thing is bad for you. Just because you're eating a salad does not necessarily make it healthy if you eat 3 pounds of it every day. So, mix it up, and have some variety.

• The average daily limit on calories is 2,500 for males

and 2,000 for females of average body size. Read up on how to best divide that amount of calories for your meals within a day. Some like to have 5 to 6 small meals throughout, while some like to have a single big one. Do what is best for you and your body.

• The recipes under this section are nutrient-dense but low calories, so test out what you like and mix and match them throughout your day.

• Once in a while, like every week or two, do indulge in a cheat meal. Have some sweets or snacks, but do not stray away from your target calorie count. Some people only eat a single meal for their cheat day, so they can eat a whole feast.

## 4.5.1 Avocado Sardines Spread

Sardines are commonly overlooked as being part of a healthy diet. They are full of complete and lean proteins, perfect for your everyday needs. They are also flavorful, so a little bit goes a long way. Coupled with the healthy fatty acids from avocado, this provides a well-balanced meal.

Ingredients:

- 7.5 oz., or 2 cans brisling sardines, in olive oil

- 1 avocado, ripe

- 2 tbsp. parsley, finely chopped

- 1 tbsp. sherry vinegar or red wine vinegar

- 1 tsp. lemon juice

- Salt and pepper to taste

Directions:

1. Drain your sardines, saving the oil. Pour about 2 tablespoons of the oil into a bowl, and then add the sherry vinegar and lemon juice. Whisk these together into a vinaigrette.

2. Cut the avocados in half, remove the seed, and scoop out the flesh into the bowl. Use a spatula or fork to mash the avocado. Mix them well so the vinaigrette can prevent the browning of the avocado.

3. Break down the sardines, remove the bones if you like, and add them into the avocado mixture. Mix it well,

transfer into 4 8 oz.-jars, and pour a layer of the sardine oil on top. Store in the fridge so the oil layer on top solidifies, preventing oxidation and drying out.

4. For consumption, simply spread the contents of a jar on a warm toast.

## 4.5.2 Overnight Oatmeal

There are numerous versions of overnight oats, so you can have a different flavor every time. This is a healthier version, loaded with fruits and nuts for vitamins, protein, and awesome flavor.

Ingredients:

- 3 cups rolled oats

- 3 cups soy milk

- 1 cup walnuts, chopped

- 1 cup sweet cherries, pitted and finely chopped

- 2 tbsp. stevia sweetener, or to your liking

- 1 ½ cup chia seeds

- 2 tsp. vanilla extract

- 1 tsp. ground cinnamon

Directions:

1. Whisk the soy milk, stevia, vanilla extract, and cinnamon in a bowl until the stevia and cinnamon are fully dissolved.

2. Add the oats, chia seeds, walnuts and cherries. Mix them well, and then distribute among the jars. Close the lid, and stash in the fridge. Wait for a full day before eating a jar.

## 4.5.3 Zucchini Noodles Puttanesca

Pasta is nice and good, but they do pack quite a bit of carbs, which translates to having quite a bit of calories on them. Most of the nutrition from pasta dishes comes from the sauce that goes with them, so why not keep the sauce and exchange the pasta for something more nutrient-dense? That's where the zucchini comes in! We are making this recipe with simple yet exquisite puttanesca ingredients.

Ingredients:

- 2 large zucchinis

- 1 lb. plum tomatoes, peeled and quartered

- 4 garlic cloves, finely grated

- 3 anchovy filets, chopped fine

- ½ cup black olives, sliced

- 3 tbsp. olive oil

- 2 tbsp. capers, finely chopped

- 1 tbsp. dried basil

- 1 tbsp. dried oregano

- Salt and pepper to taste

Directions:

1. Use a vegetable spiralizer to cut your zucchinis into noodles. If you don't have that fancy gadget, you can simply use a Y-peeler and shave off really thin strips of

zucchini. You will have wide noodles, though. Set these aside.

2. Set a wide pan or wok over medium-low heat and add the olive oil. It's healthy and will form part of the sauce, so it's alright to use this amount. Immediately add the anchovies and garlic while the oil is still cool, and let it cook slowly.

3. Once the garlic has browned, add the tomatoes and mix thoroughly. Bring up the heat to medium-high so the water from the tomatoes can evaporate. Cook for about 10 minutes, pressing the tomatoes with your spoon or spatula to break them down.

4. Add the olive and capers, and bring the heat back down again to simmer for another 10 minutes. Give it a taste and season with salt and pepper. Take it off the heat.

5. Stuff your zucchini noodles in your jars, and pour the sauce over. Sprinkle on the basil and oregano. Let it completely cool before putting on the lid and storing in the fridge. You can heat it in the microwave before eating or eat it straight-up chilled.

# 4.5.4 Zucchini Lasagna

Since we are using zucchini as pasta, why not make a ketogenic version of the classic lasagna? It's meaty, cheesy, and downright filling. Mangia!

Ingredients:

- 1 large zucchini

- 1 lb. ground turkey or chicken

- ½ cup tomato paste

- 2 cup mozzarella

- 2 tbsp. Italian seasoning

- 1 small onion, finely chopped

- 2 cloves of garlic, finely grated

- Salt and pepper to taste

Directions:

1. Use a kitchen mandolin, and slice your zucchini as

thin as you can. Set these aside.

2. Set a wide pan or wok over medium-low heat and add a bit of oil. Sauté the onion and garlic until fragrant and the onion is translucent.

3. Add the ground chicken or turkey and slightly brown them. Add the tomato paste and Italian seasoning, and mix everything well. Add just enough water to adjust the consistency into a really thick sauce. Do not make it watery and loose. Give it a taste, and season accordingly. Take it off the heat and let it cool completely to room temperature

4. To assemble, place a thin layer of the sauce at the bottom, and then layer on the zucchini and the cheese. Repeat this sequence once or twice more, adding extra cheese at the top. You can sprinkle on more Italian seasoning if you like. Close the lid, and store in the fridge.

5. To reheat, let the jar come up to room temperature, open it up, and then zap in the microwave for a few minutes until the cheese is melted. Be careful, it will be hot.

# 4.5.5 Purple Power Potion

Most Americans have really busy mornings and can't even sit down and have a proper breakfast. This recipe packs enough nutrients to get your morning started, and you can just drink it from your mason jar as you go to work.

Ingredients:

- 1 cup soy milk

- 1 cup fresh orange juice

- 2 large bananas, chopped and frozen

- 1 cup frozen strawberries

- 1 cup frozen blueberries

- 1 cup frozen peaches

Directions:

Place everything in the pitcher of your blender and process until smooth. Distribute them among your jars and stash in the fridge. Before you drink, be sure to give it a good shake first since the solids can settle and the milk can separate.

## 4.6 Dried Meals in Jars

If there is a nearby dried goods supplier near your area, or you're one of those blessed with a home dehydrator, then this section is for you. These jarred meals make use of dehydrated ingredients, which makes it easier to mix and store for a long time. Doing this makes it feel like you are eating in the army or up in the space station with the astronauts. Dried meals will last for many years and can even withstand space travel, making it perfect for long term storage or as emergency rations. You just have to rehydrate them for a nice warm meal.

• Now, there are several dehydrated food brands, and you can even dehydrate food yourself. Each ingredient also dehydrates differently. So, always check on the equivalent amount when rehydrated on your dehydrated food packaging. Other than amounts, feel free to play around with the ratios to your liking.

• The layered dried goods in a jar sure do look good.

This style allows you to identify what is in the jar and also makes for lovely gifts. However, when storing them, place them in a cool, dry place away from light, as light can cause damage to food.

• When opening up the packages of your dried ingredients, make sure to assemble all your jarred meals within a day or 2. Opening up a package of dried food or ingredients and taking out what you need introduces oxygen inside the pack. If you have any leftovers from your jarred dried food, it's best to also place an oxygen absorber in the original packaged dried ingredient.

• Make sure you include a food oxygen absorber in the jar or vacuum seal the jars with a food saver. This is imperative to put all dried foods in a jar.

• In case you are forgetful, like me, you can make reheating instructions on stickers and stick it on the jars so that you will know how to rehydrate the recipe. It also provides guidance in case you are handing out the jars as gifts.

## 4.6.1 Dry Mac and Cheese

For this recipe, most of the dehydrated products are

already available in a conventional grocery store. However, if you want a better version, you can add some dehydrated meat and vegetables to it.

Ingredients:

- 1 lb. dry elbow macaroni

- 1 cup cheese powder

- 3 tbsp. milk powder

- 2 tbsp. butter powder

- ½ tsp. salt

- ½ tsp ground black pepper

Directions:

1. Divide the macaroni into 4 jars. Mix the cheese, milk, and butter powders into a bowl, and sprinkle on some salt and pepper. Mix it well, then divide it into 4 small plastic bags. Place a bag in each jar, drop in an oxygen absorber, and seal.

2. To cook, simply take the bag out, and pour the

macaroni in a pot. Cover with an inch of water, and then set over medium heat to boil. After about 5 to 7 minutes, the pasta should be tender, with some water left in the pot. Pour the contents of the flavor pack, and mix well to rehydrate. Add more water if it gets too dry.

## 4.6.2 Homemade Pancake Mix

Craving for some flapjacks, but you feel that measuring stuff and mixing them up is too much work, particularly in the early hours of the morning? Then, a pancake mix is the answer! No, I'm not talking about those mixes that you pick up in the grocery store with disappointing sheets of dough. I'm talking about authentic home-cooked pancakes here - we are just pre-mixing the dry stuff for easy preparation and cooking.

Ingredients:

- 8 cups all-purpose flour

- 2 tbsp. sugar

- 1 ½ tbsp. baking powder

- 1 ½ tbsp. salt

- 2 tsp. baking soda

- 2 cups milk

- 2 large eggs

Directions:

1. Mix the flour, sugar, baking powder, salt, and baking soda in a large bowl and gently whisk them together. Make sure everything is well distributed.

2. Portion the pancake mix by placing 2 cups of it in each jar. Seal them tight and place them in the cupboard or pantry for storage.

3. To cook, simply mix 1 jar of pancake mix with 2 eggs and 2 cups of milk. Cook in a buttered skillet, and stack them high! You can have them with syrup, fruits, more butter, bacon, ham, or sausages.

## 4.6.3 Fruity Oats

If you've ever bought a package of instant oats with fruits, you were likely disappointed when you cooked it and saw that wasn't much fruit in it (just lots of sugar).

We can remedy that by making our own. You can eat as much fruit as you want and even pick out which fruits to add.

Ingredients:

- 2 cups instant oats

- ½ cup raisin, dehydrated, not sun-dried

- ½ cup dehydrated apples

- 1 tbsp. brown sugar

- 1 tsp. ground cinnamon

Directions:

1. Mix everything up, and divide into 4 jars. Add an oxygen absorber in the jar and seal.

2. To cook, pour the contents into a bowl, and pour on hot water. Adjust the amount of water to the consistency that you like.

# 4.6.4 Beef Paella

A nice filling dish with lively and slightly spicy flavors. It's great for impressing your surprise guests. Who says emergency foods should be boring?

Ingredients:

- 6 cups long grain rice

- 3 cups freeze-dried ground beef

- 3 cups freeze-dried ground pork

- ½ cup freeze-dried bell pepper

- ½ cup freeze-dried onion

- ½ cup freeze-dried corn kernels

- 2 tbsp. dried hot chilies, choose any variety that you like

- 1 tbsp. freeze-dried garlic granules

- ½ cup tomato powder

- 1 tbsp. smoked paprika

- 6 bay leaves

Directions:

1. Layer all of the ingredients into 6 jars, starting off with the paprika, tomato powder, and garlic at the bottom. Seal and store in your pantry.

2. To cook, pour the contents into a large skillet or pot, and pour in about 3 cups of water. Set over medium-low heat, and simmer for about 25 to 30 minutes or until the rice is tender.

## 4.6.5 Green Bean Casserole

An American comfort food classic - plus, it's tasty and healthy too. This may not be the green bean casserole that your grandma used to make, but it does the job and is actually good.

Ingredients:

- 6 cups freeze-dried green beans

- 3 cups freeze-dried mushrooms

- 1 cup freeze-dried onion

- ½ cup milk powder

- ¼ cup butter powder

- 1 tbsp. freeze-dried garlic granules

- 2 tbsp. salt

- 2 tbsp. ground black pepper

Directions:

1. Mix the milk powder, butter powder, garlic, salt and black pepper in a bowl, and distribute among 6 jars. Layer the green beans, mushroom, and onion. Seal and store in your pantry.

2. To cook, pour the contents into a large skillet or pot, and pour in about a cup of water. Set over medium-low heat, and simmer for about 10 minutes. Adjust the water amount depending on the consistency that you like.

# 4.6.6 Lentil Soup

Lentils are a great legume. It has a good amount of carbohydrates, fiber, and a menagerie of nutrients. It's a powerful ingredient that is a good addition to any meal. Lentil soups are warming, particularly on a cold night, and are just a delight to have. It's easy to make too.

Ingredients:

- 6 cups dried lentils, green or red

- 3 cups dried split peas

- 1 cup dehydrated onion

- 4 tbsp. powdered broth, you can use chicken or powdered vegetable broth for a vegetarian option

- 1 tbsp. dried basil

- 1 tbsp. dried sage

- Salt and pepper

Directions:

1. Mix the powdered broth, basil, and sage. If the powdered broth you used has no salt or is low on sodium, you may add some salt and pepper. Mix it well, and distribute among 6 jars.

2. Layer on the lentils, split peas, and onion among the jars. Add the oxygen absorbers, and seal it up.

3. To cook, empty the contents of the jar into a pot, and add about 2 cups of water. Simmer until the lentils are tender.

# 5 I Got Canned!

When talking about meals in jars, one can't go through a whole book without talking about home canning. The term may refer to cans, but home canners and the government all agree that mason jars are the best way to preserve food at home. You read that right - the earlier recipes in this book make use of the beloved mason jars as temporary storage, carrying vessels, or even eating vessels. However, its true potential lies in preservation. You can actually store food in mason jars for months without refrigeration.

It's not as simple as jamming food in a jar and closing the lid, though. Canning requires a special process to ensure the cleanliness and sanitation of the jars and the food inside them, allowing preservation.

## 5.1 Why Can with Jars

Canned goods might have flooded our markets, but there is still a benefit to canning at home. That is why it's still practiced to this day, and the government even gives out recipes and pointers on how to properly do it. Canning takes making meals in jars to another level. This is where boys and girls become men and women. So, let's look at the benefits of home canning.

• Preserving food is a good hobby to have. It allows you to fully utilize the food that you buy and can even improve its flavor. If you are a doomsday prepper, then you can start stocking up now, and you will be set for a long time. You may also do what I do, which is stock up my pantry as much as it can hold, and every time I finish a certain amount of my canned meals, I just replace them with a new batch. Just follow the mantra of "first in, first out."

• Receiving store-bought canned goods may not be

appealing to a lot of people, but home canning makes it more worthwhile. You are almost assured that the food is prepared with tender love and care, or at least with more freedom and better ingredients than industrially made canned goods. They are good for moving-in gifts, potlucks, holiday giveaways, or even just for sharing meals. Plus, who can resist those cute, sturdy, and highly decorative mason jars?

• Preserving food allows you to enjoy produce at its peak flavor any time of the year, even, and particularly, when they are out of season. Do you want to enjoy summer asparagus in autumn or spring tomatoes in winter? Canning is the way to go. You can also extend your enjoyment of some highly perishable goods by preserving them in canning, which leads us to...

• Home canning helps in reducing food waste. You can buy produce in bulk, prepare what you can eat within a week or two, and just preserve the rest. No spoilage and the producers get to move all of their products. It's great for your household waste generation, the producer's waste generation, and it also leads to the best reason why I like jarred meals, which is...

• Saving money. Buying in bulk allows you to get items at a discount, particularly when the produce is in season and at its peak quality. So, there's no waste, and you get to enjoy every cent that you paid for, getting the most bang for your back. You should also check out the local producers, farms, or markets near your area. Since they don't incur a lot of transportation and handling expenses, they will charge cheaper for their products, and you can help them with their business by being patrons.

## 5.2 Tools of the Can

Aside from the obvious mason jars, we will need some added tools to can food properly. It will take a bit of investment, but if you ask me, it's worth it since you will be preserving food for a long time.

• We are now in the realm of canning, and it's here where things get quite delicate. You will need some more equipment. First, you will need a vessel that can accommodate all your jars for sanitizing as well as sealing. You may use a really large pot, but you will be limited to the water bath and steam canning method. If you can spare some cash, you can get a pressure canner which can handle water bath, steam, and pressure canning.

o A water bath canner looks similar to a regular stock pot, as you will submerge the jars, lids and all into the hot water and boil them for a certain amount of time before cooling down and storing.

o A steam canner looks similar, but it has a compartment at the bottom to be filled with a specific amount of water. This is then boiled and allowed to steam the jars within. A heavy lid traps all the steam and heat inside as it kills off the bacteria. It requires less water compared to a water bath canner, but it also runs the risk of drying out if you leave it too long, as some recipes require, so you will have to match it with the type of recipe.

o A pressure canner looks like a cross between a large pot and a pressure cooker. You will not need to fully submerge the jars, but you need more than enough water for the whole cooking and sterilization process. This is usually employed for meats and non-acidic foods since they require a higher temperature than the boiling point to kill off the harmful bacteria and microorganisms.

• When you buy a canner, it usually comes with a

canning rack or basket that will keep your jars raised and will keep them away from the direct heat that will be coming from the bottom released by your stove. This is to avoid breakage. The bubbles formed during boiling can also rock your jars back and forth and can crack them up, so this spacer is necessary. If you are not getting a new canner and instead are using a large pot, you may retrofit spacers by using cooling racks, steamer baskets, or fry baskets. Just keep in mind that it should keep the jars from touching the bottom of the pot and should provide a stable surface for the jars to stand on.

• Since canning involves heat, you will need a thermometer to get accurate readings when sanitizing and sealing up your jars. The thermometer is also handy in measuring the temperature of your food, as some recipes require them to be at certain temperatures before they go into the jars.

• Again, since we are dealing with heat, you will need some canning tongs or jar lifters to handle the hot and heavy jars in and out of the canner. Believe me - the last thing you want is 200°F shards of glass and soup flying all around you.

• For sanitation, always have a pack of paper towels nearby for wiping off smudges that can be breeding grounds for molds and bacteria and for drying off the lids and rings. When cooking with kids, have hand sanitizer or rubbing alcohol nearby, and teach the children the importance of cleanliness when working around food. Teach them the all-important concept of cleaning after themselves and proper equipment handling. Of course, you should still do the heavy lifting, figuratively and literally.

## 5.3 Way of the Can

As with the investment in the canning equipment, you will need to invest a bit of your time too. However, you can think of it like this - it takes the same amount of time and effort to can a single jar of food as canning as many jars your canner can handle. So, you can devote a few hours of your day to process several jars that can feed you for several days or during emergencies.

Now, there are mainly 2 canning processes employed by the typical American home canner. First is the water bath canning and the steam canning. Yes, there are 2 of them, but since they essentially have the same function, I usually consider them under a single type. Essentially, the jars containing the food are exposed to an environment with a temperature of 212°F, the boiling point of water. This temperature is enough to kill the harmful bacteria within the food, as well as on the surface of the jar and lid. At this heat level, the air inside the jar expands, forcing it out of the vessel. This temperature also melts the sealing compound manufactured under the lid, which is designed to hermetically seal the jar. When it cools down, the air molecules revert to their usual distance between each other, creating a vacuum within the headspace of the jar, giving them a distinctive pop when being opened for the first time.

The process just differs in the environment that sterilizes the jars. The water bath canning process is done by fully submerging the jars and heating them up. This is a highly efficient process, but it does use up a lot of water and a lot more energy to bring it up to temperature. Steam canning, on the other hand, uses less water and instead envelopes the jars in the hot steam to sterilize them. It's a certified method and works really well since it uses less water and less energy to boil them with. However, for canned goods that have a processing time of over 45 minutes, you run the risk of drying out in the steam canner, and this can give you bad results.

When you are attempting water bath or steam canning, remember that just because the water is bubbling, it doesn't necessarily mean that it's at 212°F. Particularly for those at an altitude of 2,000 ft above sea level (ASL), water boils at a lower temperature because of less air pressure in the atmosphere, so make sure to use a thermometer. Another caveat to water bath and steam canning, and I think this is the most important one, is that these processes only work for highly acidic food, like jams, sauce, and pickles. The boiling temperature only kills certain types of bacteria, but the main problem with canning is the Clostridium botulinum - which causes botulism to anyone who ingests them - that's only affected by acidity or a higher heat.

Now, my goal in this book is to have meals in jars, and for that, we need something more powerful to fight against botulism. The best way to get temperatures higher than 212°F is by adding pressure. The super high temperature kills off any harmful bacteria, including C. botulinum. So, let's concentrate on how to process the jars with a pressure canner. Here are the steps to do proper pressure canning:

1. First, you will have to clean your jars. Unlike water bath or steam canning, which dictates sterilizing the jars for 10 minutes in boiling water, pressure canning only requires a good scrub with warm water and soap before thoroughly rinsing with more warm water. The excessive heat in the pressure canner will take care of the rest. Make sure to clean the lids and screw bands as well, and dry them properly on a rack before using them.

2. Before doing any canning, you should read your pressure canner's manual. It typically has markings inside that sets the operating water line. Pour water up to that level, and set it on the stove.

3. When filling your jars, use a very clean jar funnel to avoid spillage and keep the rims clean. The recipes I've used here require an inch of headspace, but if you are trying out other recipes, refer to the required headspace. Before placing the lids, you can wipe the rim to make sure there are no morsels of food, drops of sauce, or moisture on them. Wear some gloves, or use kitchen tongs, to handle the clean lids and place them on top of the jars. Secure the screw bands around the lid, but do not over-tighten them. Finger-tight will suffice to allow for air from inside to escape and to make room for the metal's

expansion when heated.

4. Check the temperatures before putting your jars in the canner. If you put hot food into the jar, it will naturally heat up the glass, and if you put the warm glass in cold water, it can cause cracks. Match the temperature of the glass to the temperature of the water in the canner when you place them. Also, place the canner rack or spacer before the jars since it also needs to warm up. The rack is important since it prevents the jars from touching the bottom of the canner, where the vapor will bubble up and can knock the jars over.

5. Carefully place the jars in the canner, and set the heat source to medium-high. This will bring up the temperature without shocking the jars. Lock in the lid.

6. Now, depending on the brand and model of your pressure canner, it should have safety and functional features, so check your manual. Most pressure canners have a gauge so you can check the pressure. Some have a vent that is closed by a flap or weight, but you should keep this open for now. Allow the canner to vent for 10 to 15 minutes to make sure that the correct operating temperature is reached and the cold air has been

expunged. Some pressure canner models have a pin that pops up when the correct temperature has been reached, even when venting.

7. Once the canner has vented and the lock is properly secured, you may put on the weighted valve or close the vent with the heat still on medium-high. The typical canning pressure is 11 to 15 pounds per square inch (psi), adding 1 psi over 11 for every 2,000 ft. increase above 2,000 ft. ASL mark.

8. When the pressure has reached 5 or 6 psi, you may begin to lower the heat to medium to heat things slowly and to not overshoot the pressure. Remember, we are still working with glass here, so some care should be observed. When it reaches 9 or 10 psi, lower the heat to medium-low until it reaches 11, and maintain it there.

9. When the target psi has been reached, only then should you start the timer for processing. The usual processing time for pint (16 oz.) jars is 1 hour and 15 minutes, and for quart (32 oz.) jars, it's 1 hour and 30 minutes. During the processing time, particularly if it's your first time to pressure can, keep an eye on the pressure gauge and make sure it stays on target. If it dips

a bit, you will need to increase the temperature a bit to reach the pressure again and restart the timer. So, watch it carefully. When you have gained some experience and you are really familiar with your pressure canner and stove, then you can just check on it every 20 to 30 minutes.

10. If you have ever seen someone cook with a pressure cooker before, I bet that after the cooking time, they open up the vent or place the whole pressure cooker in the sink and under running water. We are not doing that here. After the processing time, simply turn off the heat, and leave it alone. Let the temperature and pressure come down by itself. Opening up the vent will drastically change the environment and blow up the jars. So, take your time.

11. When the pressure has gone down completely, open up the vents. Unlock the lid, but you can keep it ajar as the jars cool down more. You can see that the liquid contents are still bubbling, and this can be dangerous if you move them. Leave them alone for about 10 to 20 more minutes.

12. When things have settled down a bit, grab a baking

dish or tray lined with a kitchen towel. This will be your resting and cooling rack.

13. Use your jar lifters, attach them securely under the screw band, lift up a jar, and place it on your resting rig. Repeat with the rest, being careful that they don't hit each other. You may inspect them for any leaks or failed seals, but do not touch them overnight for the seal to fully adhere. You can cover them with more kitchen towels if you want to avoid getting dirt or bacteria on them.

14. After the resting period, fully sealed jars can now be stored in the pantry. It is, however, advised to remove the screw bands before storing. This prevents the screw bands from rusting while in contact with the rim and lid of the canned food you worked hard on. Removing the screw bands also makes it easier for you to inspect for failed seals, but do not turn the jar upside down or on its side, as the seals are still curing for several days. Besides, home canned goods are better when consumed a few weeks after canning. If you have some failed seals, you may transfer them to your fridge for storage, but make sure to consume them within the next few days.

# 5.4 Canning Recipes

The recipes here are formulated and approved by the United States Department of Agriculture (USDA) and the National Center for Home Food Preservation (NCHFP). Canning requires sterilization and proper processing to prevent the growth of harmful - and some fatal - bacteria and to ensure that the canned food can last several months, even a year, in the pantry without spoilage. Let's get canning!

## 5.4.1 Canned Pea Soup

Canned pea soups need not be boring anymore! You can make this recipe a vegetarian option if you like, or you can add ham and some grilled meat to it for a meatier soup. No matter how you take it, it goes well with some warm buttered toast.

Ingredients:

- 8 cups vegetable broth, you might need more or less to properly fill up the jars

- 2 cups dry split peas

- 1 ½ cup ham, cooked and cut into bite-sized pieces (optional if you are going vegan)

- 1 cup carrots, finely chopped

- 1 cup onion, finely chopped

- 3 garlic cloves, finely chopped

- 2 tbsp. curry powder

- 1 tbsp. Worcestershire sauce, or ½ tbsp soy sauce and ½ tbsp. apple cider vinegar if you are going vegan

- 1 bay leaf

- Salt and pepper to taste

* This recipe is for 5 16-oz. jars and processed in a pressure canner.

Directions:

1. Pour the peas into a pot, and add just enough vegetable broth to cover them by about a quarter of an inch. Set over medium-low heat, and bring to a bare simmer. Cook for 50 minutes, then add the carrots and

cook for a further 10 minutes. As you are cooking the peas, it will be a good idea to set up your pressure canner. Clean your jars as well.

2. Take a stick blender and puree the peas and carrots, adding more vegetable broth if it gets too dry. We are looking for a loose slurry. Return it to medium-low heat.

3. Add the rest of the ingredients, simmer for about 30 minutes, and give it a taste. Season with salt and pepper, and fish out the bay leaf.

4. Distribute the soup among your jars, and fill up the space with the extra vegetable broth. However, do keep an inch of head space available to allow for the expansion of liquid.

5. Place the lids on the jars, using tongs or a gloved hand, and screw on the metal rings. Add a bit of water into the pressure canner, and try to heat it up to the same temperature as the jars to prevent cracking. Place the jars in and adjust the water level as the pressure canner suggests. Close and lock the lid, but keep the vent open. Bring to a boil, allowing the steam to come out of the vent for 10 minutes.

6. After venting the pressure canner, close the vents, and set it to hold 10 lbs. of pressure for a weighted-gauge pressure canner and 11 lbs. of pressure for a dial-gauge pressure canner. Please increase pressure by 1 lb. for every 2,000 feet over the 2,000 feet mark, above sea level, for your area. If you are using a weighted-gauge pressure canner, then just use the 15 lb. vent weight if you are in an area above 2,000 feet above sea level.

7. Let the pressure build up, adjusting the heat to maintain the pressure, and then set the timer for 1 hour and 15 minutes, no less.

8. After the processing time, turn off the heat, but do not open the vent. Let the pressure come down for 45 minutes. If your indicator says that here is no more pressure left inside, wait for another 2 minutes to be sure.

9. After waiting, open up the vent, and let it cool down for another 10 minutes before you open the lid. Have a baking tray lined with a kitchen towel ready. Gently remove the jars, one by one, and place them on the cooling rig. Do not move the jars after placing them on the cooling rig for 12 to 24 hours, so the seal can fully adhere and cool down. You may then remove the rings and inspect for

leaks or gaps. If you have found any, transfer the jar to your fridge and consume within a week or so. The rest may be moved to the pantry for storage.

## 5.4.2 Canned Pork (Sausage) and Beans

It's very comforting to have a nice bowl of beans on a cold winter night, and this recipe can give you that in case you are snowed in. This is a hearty meal that warms you up and fills you up really well.

Ingredients:

• 4 cups pork or chicken broth; you might need more or less to properly fill up the jars

• 1 lb. sausages of your choice, like Hungarian, chorizo, or Italian, sliced into bite-sized pieces

• 1 cup dried beans of your choice, like black eyed peas, pinto, or white beans

• 2 celery stalks, cut into bite-sized pieces

• 1 cup carrots, finely chopped

- 1 cup onion, finely chopped

- 4 garlic cloves, finely chopped

- 1 tbsp. ground fennel seeds

- 2 bay leaves

- Salt and pepper to taste

* This recipe is for 6 16-oz. jars and processed in a pressure canner.

Directions:

1. Give the beans a rinse, and remove any debris or bad beans. Transfer into a pot and cover with 2 inches of water. Set over medium heat and bring to a boil. Once boiling, adjust the heat to maintain a bare simmer. Cook this covered for 30 minutes. We are not looking for the beans to be tender - just slightly soft since they will cook more in the canning process.

2. Drain the beans and set them aside. Return the pot over medium heat and dry it off. When it's completely dried, add a bit of oil and add the sliced sausages. Cook

until perfectly browned. Remove the sausage slices to drain.

3. Using the same pot, add more oil if necessary; otherwise, dump in the celery, carrots, onion, and garlic. Sauté them, picking up the fond that gets stuck at the bottom from frying the sausages.

4. When the vegetables have sweated and have developed a bit of color, deglaze with about 2 cups of the broth, and scrape the bottom to remove any stuck bits. Add the bay leaves and beans. Mix these well, and simmer for 10 minutes. Give it a taste and season with salt and pepper. Fish out the bay leaves after cooking. Set up your pressure canner, and clean your jars.

5. Distribute the sausage pieces into the jars so that they will not crumble, and then pour in the warm bean mixture. Give it a few taps on the side or the counter to get rid of any air pockets. Leave an inch of headspace in each jar, filling it up with more broth if needed.

6. Place the lids on the jars using tongs or a gloved hand, and screw on the metal rings. Add a bit of water into the pressure canner, and try to heat it up to the same temperature as the jars. Place the jars in and adjust the

water level as the pressure canner suggests. Close and lock the lid, but keep the vent open. Bring to a boil, allowing the steam to come out of the vent for 10 minutes.

7. After venting the pressure canner, close the vents, and set it to hold 10 lbs. of pressure for a weighted-gauge pressure canner and 11 lbs. of pressure for a dial-gauge pressure canner. Please increase pressure by 1 lb. for every 2,000 feet over the 2,000 feet mark, above sea level, for your area. If you are using a weighted-gauge pressure canner, then just use the 15 lb. vent weight if you are in an area above 2,000 feet above sea level.

8. Let the pressure build up, adjusting the heat to maintain the pressure. And then set the timer for 1 hour, no less.

9. After the processing time, turn off the heat, but do not open the vent. Let the pressure come down for 45 minutes. If your indicator says that there is no more pressure left inside, wait for another 2 minutes to be sure.

10. After waiting, open up the vent, and let it cool down for another 10 minutes before you open the lid. Have a baking tray lined with a kitchen towel ready. Gently remove the jars one by one, and place them on the cooling

rig. Do not move the jars after placing them on the cooling rig for 12 to 24 hours so the seal can fully adhere and cool down. You may then remove the rings and inspect for leaks or gaps. If you have found any, transfer the jar to your fridge and consume within a week or so. The rest may be moved to the pantry for storage.

## 5.4.3 Canned Chicken Soup

A chicken soup not just for the soul but for the tummy as well. You can have it as a ready-to-eat microwaveable meal or heat it up on the stove with some pasta or dried noodles and go to town with it. It's nutritious and delicious.

Ingredients:

• 6 cups chicken broth, you might need more or less to properly fill up the jars

• 3 lbs. chicken breasts, boneless and skinless, cut into bite-sized chunks

• ½ cup potato, peeled and diced

• ½ cup carrots, diced

- ¼ cup corn kernels, frozen is fine

- ¼ cup green peas, frozen is also fine

- 2 tbsp. dried thyme

- Salt and pepper to taste

* This recipe is for 6 16-oz. jars and processed in a pressure canner.

Directions:

1. Set a pot over medium heat, and add a bit of oil. When the oil is hot, add the chicken chunks, and sprinkle on a bit of salt. Sauté this until the chicken has developed a bit of color. It's fine if they are still pink or raw inside.

2. Drain some excess oil if needed, and then pour in about 4 cups of chicken broth. Scrape the bottom to loosen up any stuck bits. Bring to a boil, and then lower the heat to maintain a bare simmer. Add the potato, carrots, and thyme, and let everything cook for about 5 minutes.

3. After 5 minutes, add the corn and peas, and let it warm up for another 5 minutes. Set the soup aside, and

set up the pressure canner and jars.

4. Use a slotted spoon or a ladle with holes to scoop up the solids and distribute them among your jars. Pour in the soup, leaving only an inch of headspace. Add more warmed-up chicken broth if needed. Give it a gentle shake to release any air pockets that may have been trapped.

5. Place the lids on the jars using tongs or a gloved hand, and screw on the metal rings. Add a bit of water into the pressure canner, and try to heat it up to the same temperature as the jars. Place the jars in, and adjust the water level as the pressure canner suggests. Close and lock the lid, but keep the vent open. Bring to a boil, allowing the steam to come out of the vent for 10 minutes.

6. After venting the pressure canner, close the vents and set it to hold 10 lbs. of pressure for a weighted-gauge pressure canner and 11 lbs. of pressure for a dial-gauge pressure canner. Please increase pressure by 1 lb. for every 2,000 feet over the 2,000 feet mark, above sea level, for your area. If you are using a weighted-gauge pressure canner, then just use the 15 lb. vent weight if you are in an area above 2,000 feet above sea level.

7. Let the pressure build up, adjusting the heat to

maintain the pressure, and then set the timer for 1 hour and 30 minutes, no less.

8. After the processing time, turn off the heat, but do not open the vent. Let the pressure come down for 45 minutes. If your indicator says that there is no more pressure left inside, wait for another 2 minutes to be sure.

9. After waiting, open up the vent and let it cool down for another 10 minutes before you open the lid. Have a baking tray lined with a kitchen towel ready. Gently remove the jars one by one and place them on the cooling rig. Do not move the jars after placing them on the cooling rig for 12 to 24 hours, so the seal can fully adhere and cool down. You may then remove the rings and inspect for leaks or gaps. If you have found any, transfer the jar to your fridge and consume within a week or so. The rest may be moved to the pantry for storage.

## 5.4.4 Asparagus Soup

Asparagus is one of those crops that are only good for a relatively small portion of the year. That is why people go nuts over them when they are in season, particularly the Germans with their white asparagus. Canning allows you to get good in-season asparagus and yet enjoy them any time you like. Here's an asparagus soup recipe that is delectable and great for enjoying even outside the asparagus season.

Ingredients:

- 6 cups vegetable broth, you might need more or less to properly fill up the jars

- 3 lbs. asparagus, woody root segments removed, and roughly chopped

- 2 celery stalks, cut into chunks

- 1 large onion, cut into quarters

- 1 whole head or garlic, peeled and lightly crushed

- ½ cup butter

- ½ cup chives, finely chopped

- 1 tbsp. lime juice

- Salt and pepper to taste

* This recipe is for 6 16-oz. jars and processed in a

pressure canner.

Directions:

1. Set a pot over medium heat, and drop in the butter, celery, onion, and garlic. Sauté until the onion is translucent. Add the asparagus and mix everything well, cooking for about 10 minutes.

2. Add the broth and bring to a boil. Lower the heat to maintain a bare simmer, and cook for about an hour. Set up your pressure canner and jars as the soup cooks.

3. After cooking time, add the lime juice and chives. Use a stick blender or your food processor and puree everything. Give it a taste and season accordingly. Do not thicken the soup with starch or flour. You may thicken just before serving but never before canning, as it disrupts heat absorption and can prevent the killing of bacteria. Distribute the soup among the jars, leaving an inch of headspace.

4. Place the lids on the jars using tongs or a gloved hand, and screw on the metal rings. Add a bit of water into the pressure canner and try to heat it up to the same temperature as the jars. Place the jars in and adjust the

water level as the pressure canner suggests. Close and lock the lid, but keep the vent open. Bring to a boil, allowing the steam to come out of the vent for 10 minutes.

5. After venting the pressure canner, close the vents and set it to hold 10 lbs. of pressure for a weighted-gauge pressure canner and 11 lbs. of pressure for a dial-gauge pressure canner. Please increase pressure by 1 lb. for every 2,000 feet over the 2,000 feet mark, above sea level, for your area. If you are using a weighted-gauge pressure canner, then just use the 15 lb. vent weight if you are in an area above 2,000 feet above sea level.

6. Let the pressure build up, adjusting the heat to maintain the pressure, and then set the timer for 1 hour, no less.

7. After the processing time, turn off the heat, but do not open the vent. Let the pressure come down for 45 minutes. If your indicator says that there is no more pressure left inside, wait for another 2 minutes to be sure.

8. After waiting, open up the vent, and let it cool down for another 10 minutes before you open the lid. Have a baking tray lined with a kitchen towel ready. Gently remove the jars one by one, and place them on the cooling

rig. Do not move the jars after placing them on the cooling rig for 12 to 24 hours, so the seal can fully adhere and cool down. You may then remove the rings and inspect for leaks or gaps. If you have found any, transfer the jar to your fridge and consume within a week or so. The rest may be moved to the pantry for storage.

## 5.4.5 Canned Chili

If you want something heartier, meatier, and a more comforting meal, then you can never go wrong with some good chili con carne. You can make it as spicy as you want, but pair it with some dinner rolls, tortilla chips, or cornbread, and it will be a good day.

Ingredients:

• 4 cups beef broth, you might need more or less to properly fill up the jars

• 3 lbs. ground beef or venison

• 3 cups tomatoes, cut into chunks or grated

• 6 oz. (1 can) tomato paste

- ½ cup red bell pepper, roasted and chopped

- ½ cup jalapeño pepper, roasted and chopped

- ½ head of garlic, peeled and finely chopped

- 1 ½ cups onion, finely chopped

- 1 tbsp. chili powder

- 1 tbsp. dried oregano

- 1 tbsp. ground cumin

- ½ tbsp. ground fennel seeds

- ½ tbsp. smoked paprika

- 2 tbsp. cocoa powder (regular unsweetened)

- Salt and pepper to taste

* This recipe is for 6 16-oz. jars and processed in a pressure canner.

Directions:

1. Set a pot over medium heat, and pour on a thin layer of oil. Get it hot, and then sauté the ground meat, breaking it up as you do. Cook it until it develops a bit of color. Drain some excess oil when the meat is slightly done.

2. Add the garlic, and sauté it with the meat for about a minute. Then add the tomatoes, tomato paste, peppers, onion, chili powder, oregano, cumin, fennel seeds, and paprika. Continue to sauté until it just begins to stick at the bottom of the pot.

3. Deglaze everything with about 2 cups of beef broth. Scrape the bottom to release any of the stuck bits, and mix everything well. Give it a taste, and season it well. Do not thicken the chili with starch or flour. You may thicken just before serving but never before canning, as it disrupts heat absorption and can prevent the killing of bacteria. Take it off the heat, and set up your pressure canner.

4. Distribute your chili among the jars, adding more warmed up beef broth if needed to have an inch of headspace. Give it a gentle shake to release any air pockets that may have been trapped.

5. Place the lids on the jars using tongs or a gloved

hand, and screw on the metal rings. Add a bit of water into the pressure canner, and try to heat it up to the same temperature as the jars. Place the jars in and adjust the water level as the pressure canner suggests. Close and lock the lid, but keep the vent open. Bring to a boil, allowing the steam to come out of the vent for 10 minutes.

6. After venting the pressure canner, close the vents and set it to hold 10 lbs. of pressure for a weighted-gauge pressure canner and 11 lbs. of pressure for a dial-gauge pressure canner.

7. Let the pressure build up, adjusting the heat to maintain the pressure, and then set the timer for 1 hour and 15 minutes, no less.

8. After the processing time, turn off the heat, but do not open the vent. Let the pressure come down for 45 minutes. If your indicator says that there is no more pressure left inside, wait for another 2 minutes to be sure.

9. After waiting, open up the vent, and let it cool down for another 10 minutes before you open the lid. Have a baking tray lined with a kitchen towel ready. Gently remove the jars one by one and place them on the cooling rig. Do not move the jars after placing them on the cooling

rig for 12 to 24 hours, so the seal can fully adhere and cool down. You may then remove the rings and inspect for leaks or gaps. If you have found any, transfer the jar to your fridge and consume within a week or so. The rest may be moved to the pantry for storage.

## 5.4.6 Canned Sausage and Gravy

There is just something comforting about sausages and gravy. It can be doled out over some warm biscuits, or you can even pour it into a bowl and eat it with some salad. For canning, though, you will have to thicken the gravy itself when you are reheating it by adding a slurry of flour and water.

Ingredients:

• 2 cups pork broth, you might need more or less to properly fill up the jars

• 2 cups beer

• 3 lbs. fresh sausage or ground pork, seasoned and spiced to your liking

• 2 cups potatoes, cut into bite-sized chunks; use waxy

potatoes like red potatoes or Yukon gold

- ½ head of garlic, peeled and finely chopped

- 1 ½ cups onion, finely chopped

- 1 tbsp. ground cumin

- Salt and pepper to taste

* This recipe is for 6 16-oz. jars and processed in a pressure canner.

Directions:

1. If you are using fresh sausages, cut them open and squeeze out the meat into a bowl. You can fry up the skins and have a snack. If you are going to use ground pork, transfer it into a bowl and season with salt, pepper, dried herbs, and dried ground spices.

2. Set a skillet or wide pan over medium heat, and add a bit of oil. Sauté the sausage mixture until fully cooked and browned. You can break them down for a finer texture or clump them up to make them chunky.

3. As you cook the sausage meat, set a pot over medium heat, and pour in the broth, beer, and cumin. Bring this to a bare simmer.

4. Scoop out the meat, leaving as much oil in the skillet as you can, and transfer the meat to a strainer to drain. Set the skillet back on the heat, and cook the potatoes, onion, and garlic until browned. Mix this up with the cooked sausage meat. Give the broth a taste and season accordingly. Set up your pressure canner and jars.

5. Distribute the sausage mixture among the jars, and pour on the broth, leaving an inch of headspace. Tap it a few times on the side to release any trapped air pockets.

6. Place the lids on the jars using tongs or a gloved hand, and screw on the metal rings. Add a bit of water into the pressure canner and try to heat it up to the same temperature as the jars. Place the jars in, and adjust the water level as the pressure canner suggests. Close and lock the lid, but keep the vent open. Bring to a boil, allowing the steam to come out of the vent for 10 minutes.

7. After venting the pressure canner, close the vents, and set it to hold 10 lbs. of pressure for a weighted-gauge pressure canner and 11 lbs. of pressure for a dial-gauge

pressure canner.

8. Let the pressure build up, adjusting the heat to maintain the pressure, and then set the timer for 1 hour and 15 minutes, no less.

9. After the processing time, turn off the heat, but do not open the vent. Let the pressure come down for 45 minutes. If your indicator says that there is no more pressure left inside, wait for another 2 minutes to be sure.

10. After waiting, open up the vent, and let it cool down for another 10 minutes before you open the lid. Have a baking tray lined with a kitchen towel ready. Gently remove the jars one by one and place them on the cooling rig. Do not move the jars after placing them on the cooling rig for 12 to 24 hours, so the seal can fully adhere and cool down. You may then remove the rings and inspect for leaks or gaps. If you have found any, transfer the jar to your fridge and consume within a week or so. The rest may be moved to the pantry for storage.

## 5.4.7 Canned Boeuf Bourguignon

Stews are easy meals that are improved over time, and with canning, you will certainly get the benefit of time.

This is a classic French dish made available, convenient, and quick with the joy of canning.

Ingredients:

- 2 cups beef broth, you might need more or less to properly fill up the jars

- 2 cups red wine, the cheap stuff will do fine, as long as it's drinkable

- 3 lbs. beef, cut into 2-inch cubes

- 2 cups potatoes, cut into bite-sized chunks; use waxy potatoes like red potatoes or Yukon gold

- 2 cups carrot, cut into bite-sized chunks

- ½ head of garlic, peeled and minced

- 1 ½ cups onion, finely chopped

- 4 bay leaves

- 1 tsp. dried thyme

- Salt and pepper to taste

\* This recipe is for 6 16-oz. jars and processed in a pressure canner.

Directions:

1. Set a pot over medium heat, and pour on a thin layer of oil. Get it really hot, and then sear the beef on all sides. Work in batches to get a good sear and keep the temperature of the pot high. Drain the excess oil of the beef chunks after searing each batch.

2. Remove the excess oil from the pot, keeping about a tablespoon in. Sauté the onion and garlic in the oil. Once they have developed some color, add the carrots and potatoes. Cook this for about 5 minutes.

3. Add the beef back into the pot, and deglaze with the wine. Mix everything up, scraping any stuck bits at the bottom. Bring to a simmer just to evaporate as much of the alcohol as you can for another 5 minutes. As that simmers, set up your pressure canner and jars.

4. Give your stew a taste and season with salt and pepper. Mix in the seasoning and then distribute it among the jars. Do not thicken the stew with starch or flour. You may thicken just before serving, but never before canning,

as it disrupts heat absorption and can prevent the killing of bacteria. Add more beef broth if needed to have an inch of headspace. Tap the jars to release any trapped air.

5. Place the lids on the jars using tongs or a gloved hand, and screw on the metal rings. Add a bit of water into the pressure canner and try to heat it up to the same temperature as the jars. Place the jars in and adjust the water level as the pressure canner suggests. Close and lock the lid, but keep the vent open. Bring to a boil, allowing the steam to come out of the vent for 10 minutes.

6. After venting the pressure canner, close the vents and set it to hold 10 lbs. of pressure for a weighted-gauge pressure canner and 11 lbs. of pressure for a dial-gauge pressure canner.

7. Let the pressure build up, adjusting the heat to maintain the pressure, and then set the timer for 1 hour and 15 minutes, no less.

8. After the processing time, turn off the heat, but do not open the vent. Let the pressure come down for 45 minutes. If your indicator says that there is no more pressure left inside, wait for another 2 minutes to be sure.

9. After waiting, open up the vent, and let it cool down for another 10 minutes before you open the lid. Have a baking tray lined with a kitchen towel ready. Gently remove the jars one by one and place them on the cooling rig. Do not move the jars after placing them on the cooling rig for 12 to 24 hours, so the seal can fully adhere and cool down. You may then remove the rings and inspect for leaks or gaps. If you have found any, transfer the jar to your fridge and consume within a week or so. The rest may be moved to the pantry for storage.

## 5.4.8 Canned Pasta Sauce

Pasta sauce comes in different forms, but nothing is heartier and more filling than a meat sauce. With this, you can get your meat and vegetables for the day on a single plate. Just open up a jar, reheat, thicken it if you want, and pour over some freshly cooked pasta. Just remember, a meat sauce goes well with pasta shapes that have ridges or cavities, so the chunks can go in. Also good for lasagna.

Ingredients:

- 7 lbs. tomatoes, peeled and cut into half or quarters

- 1 ½ lbs. ground beef or a medley of vegetables for a vegan option; just avoid starchy vegetables

- 1 head of garlic, finely grated

- 1 whole onion, finely chopped

- 2 large bell peppers, use your favorite color, seeded and finely chopped

- 2 large carrots, finely diced

- 2 tbsp. dried

- 2 tbsp. dried oregano

- Salt and pepper to taste

- Sugar to taste, and depending on how sweet your tomatoes are

* This recipe is for 6 16-oz. jars and processed in a pressure canner.

Directions:

1. Peel your tomatoes by blanching them in hot water

with a tiny cut on the skin. Once peeled, transfer them into a pot. Set the pot over medium heat, and sprinkle a bit of salt. Use a stick blender or a masher, and puree everything until you get a sauce. Lower the heat and maintain a bare simmer for about 10 minutes.

2. While the sauce simmers, set a skillet over medium heat and add a bit of oil. Brown the ground beef in the oil, and then add the garlic, onion, bell peppers, and carrots. Cook until the onion pieces are translucent and the carrots are slightly tender. If you are using all vegetables, sauté them in a bit of oil until they're slightly tender and have developed a bit of color.

3. Transfer the meat into the tomato sauce, and add the basil and oregano. Mix everything up, give it a taste, and season to your liking. Set up your pressure canner and jars.

4. Distribute the meat sauce among the jars. Do not thicken the sauce with starch or flour. You may thicken just before serving, but never before canning, as it disrupts heat absorption and can prevent the killing of bacteria. It's the same principle as to why we can't put in pasta when home canning. Leave an inch of headspace in

each jar.

5. Place the lids on the jars using tongs or a gloved hand, and screw on the metal rings. Add a bit of water into the pressure canner, and try to heat it up to the same temperature as the jars. Place the jars in and adjust the water level as the pressure canner suggests. Close and lock the lid, but keep the vent open. Bring to a boil, allowing the steam to come out of the vent for 10 minutes.

6. After venting the pressure canner, close the vents and set it to hold 10 lbs. of pressure for a weighted-gauge pressure canner and 11 lbs. of pressure for a dial-gauge pressure canner.

7. Let the pressure build up, adjusting the heat to maintain the pressure, and then set the timer for 1 hour, no less.

8. After the processing time, turn off the heat, but do not open the vent. Let the pressure come down for 45 minutes. If your indicator says that there is no more pressure left inside, wait for another 2 minutes to be sure.

9. After waiting, open up the vent, and let it cool down for another 10 minutes before you open the lid. Have a

baking tray lined with a kitchen towel ready. Gently remove the jars one by one and place them on the cooling rig. Do not move the jars after placing them on the cooling rig for 12 to 24 hours, so the seal can fully adhere and cool down. You may then remove the rings and inspect for leaks or gaps. If you have found any, transfer the jar to your fridge and consume within a week or so. The rest may be moved to the pantry for storage.

## 5.4.9 Canned Meatballs

I can't talk about pasta without thinking about meatballs. It might not be a classic and traditional Italian pairing, but meatballs are a good all-around (see what I did there?) food to have in a pinch. Aside from pasta applications, you can also have them in a hotdog bun or hoagie, in a wrap, or even in a salad. Meatballs are a meaty meal ready to roll into your belly!

Ingredients:

• 4 cups beef, pork, or chicken broth; you might need more or less to properly fill up the jars

• 4 lbs. ground meat, can be beef, pork, chicken, or a mixture

- 1 head of garlic, finely grated

- 2 tbsp. dried parsley

- 2 tbsp. dried thyme

- 2 tbsp. ground cumin

- 2 tbsp. ground fennel

- 2 tbsp. ground coriander seeds

- 2 bay leaves

- Salt and pepper to taste

* This recipe is for 6 16-oz. jars and processed in a pressure canner.

Directions:

1. Mix the parsley, thyme, cumin, fennel, and coriander seeds in a small bowl, and divide it into 2. Mix 1 part of the spice mixture with the ground meat, together with the grated garlic. Season with salt and pepper, and mix them well. You can take a small bit and fry it up so you can taste it. Adjust accordingly.

2. Form the meat mixture into bite-sized balls. You can go bigger, but you might have trouble fitting them into your jars. Set a skillet over medium heat, and pour in about a half inch layer of oil. At the same time, place a pot over medium heat, and pour in the broth, the remaining half of the spice mixture, and drop in the bay leaves. Bring the broth to a bare simmer.

3. When the skillet is hot, sear the meatballs until the whole surface is browned. Work in batches, placing the seared balls in a colander or cooling rack to drain any excess oil. Once you have seared all of the meatballs, set up your pressure canner and jars.

4. Distribute the meatballs among the jars, and fill it up with the warm broth, leaving an inch of headspace. Do not put the bay leaves in the jars. Give it a gentle tap if some air pockets have formed.

5. Place the lids on the jars using tongs or a gloved hand, and screw on the metal rings. Add a bit of water into the pressure canner, and try to heat it up to the same temperature as the jars. Place the jars in, and adjust the water level as the pressure canner suggests. Close and lock the lid, but keep the vent open. Bring to a boil,

allowing the steam to come out of the vent for 10 minutes.

6. After venting the pressure canner, close the vents and set it to hold 10 lbs. of pressure for a weighted-gauge pressure canner and 11 lbs. of pressure for a dial-gauge pressure canner.

7. Let the pressure build up, adjusting the heat to maintain the pressure, and then set the timer for 1 hour and 15 minutes, no less.

8. After the processing time, turn off the heat, but do not open the vent. Let the pressure come down for 45 minutes. If your indicator says that there is no more pressure left inside, wait for another 2 minutes to be sure.

9. After waiting, open up the vent, and let it cool down for another 10 minutes before you open the lid. Have a baking tray lined with a kitchen towel ready. Gently remove the jars one by one and place them on the cooling rig. Do not move the jars after placing them on the cooling rig for 12 to 24 hours, so the seal can fully adhere and cool down. You may then remove the rings and inspect for leaks or gaps. If you have found any, transfer the jar to your fridge and consume within a week or so. The rest may be moved to the pantry for storage.

# 5.4.10 Canned Chicken Pot Pie Filling

Again, I would like to remind you that home canned food is not allowed to have thickeners added to it, which is a signature feature of the chicken pot pie filling. However, this is easy to thicken and can be topped with a flaky pastry. Also, if you are quite lazy like I am and can't be bothered to buy dough and fire up the oven, you can also pour this over some microwaveable rice and zap it for a few minutes until hot, and the rice has soaked up the sauce. You can also warm it up on the stove and throw in some croutons as thickener for a hearty stew.

Ingredients:

• 4 cups chicken broth, you might need more or less to properly fill up the jars

• 1 cup white wine

• 3 lbs. chicken breast, skinless and boneless, cut into bite-sized pieces

• 1 large onion, finely chopped

• 1 cup mushrooms thinly sliced

- ½ lb. waxy potatoes, finely diced

- 1 large carrot, finely diced

- 1 cup frozen peas

- 1 tbsp. thyme

- 2 bay leaves

- Salt and pepper to taste

\* This recipe is for 6 16-oz. jars and processed in a pressure canner.

Directions:

1. Place a pot over medium heat and add a bit of oil or butter in it. Sauté the mushroom and onions in it until the onions have sweated and the mushrooms develop a bit of color.

2. Add the potato and carrot and continue to cook for about 2 minutes or until slightly tender. Then, add the chicken, peas, thyme, and bay leaf and mix everything to heat up before pouring in the wine - about 2 cups of

chicken stock. Bring to a boil, then lower the heat to maintain a bare simmer for about 10 minutes.

3. Give the stew a taste and season accordingly. Set up your pressure canner and jars. Distribute the stew among the jars, giving them a light tap or shake to get rid of any air pockets. Also, make sure that each jar gets more or less the same amount of veggies and chicken in them. I made that mistake once...Never again!

4. Place the lids on the jars using tongs or a gloved hand, and screw on the metal rings. Add a bit of water into the pressure canner, and try to heat it up to the same temperature as the jars. Place the jars in, and adjust the water level as the pressure canner suggests. Close and lock the lid, but keep the vent open. Bring to a boil, allowing the steam to come out of the vent for 10 minutes.

5. After venting the pressure canner, close the vents and set it to hold 10 lbs. of pressure for a weighted-gauge pressure canner and 11 lbs. of pressure for a dial-gauge pressure canner.

6. Let the pressure build up, adjusting the heat to maintain the pressure, and then set the timer for 1 hour and 15 minutes, no less.

7. After the processing time, turn off the heat, but do not open the vent. Let the pressure come down for 45 minutes. If your indicator says that there is no more pressure left inside, wait for another 2 minutes to be sure.

8. After waiting, open up the vent, and let it cool down for another 10 minutes before you open the lid. Have a baking tray lined with a kitchen towel ready. Gently remove the jars one by one and place them on the cooling rig. Do not move the jars after placing them on the cooling rig for 12 to 24 hours, so the seal can fully adhere and cool down. You may then remove the rings and inspect for leaks or gaps. If you have found any, transfer the jar to your fridge and consume within a week or so. The rest may be moved to the pantry for storage.

# 6 Safety First, Before You Pack Around

To reiterate what I have mentioned earlier in this book, there are 2 main ways of using jars with food. One can use jars as a form of temporary storage, lunchbox, or serving dish, and it can be treated as you would any plastic container or plate in terms of cleanliness and sanitation. The other way is for canning, which requires sterilization. Of course, we want everything to be clean, sanitized, and safe, so here are some pointers to keep in mind when you jar foods properly.

- For general storage and serving, clean your mason jars well as you would any drinking glass. You may place them in dishwashers and run the cycle. As for the lids, it's alright to place the lids and the rings in the dishwasher if the lids were already used for canning. If you are going to use the lid for canning, they should be cleaned in boiling water in the last minutes before sealing the jars. The heat from the dishwasher can soften the sealing compound and will not form an airtight seal, which is fine for regular use but not for canning.

- Mason jars can be quite sturdy. I once dropped a piece on a concrete floor, and it didn't shatter. That being said, always be careful when handling and cleaning them. They can be heavy enough to bruise and even break your toes. Broken glass shards are sharp in case you break one. Inspect for cracks before using mason jars for canning. You may wash them in cold or hot water - just don't expose them to sudden changes in temperature.

- The metal rings tend to rust over time. Even if they have a coating, it will get rubbed off from opening and closing the jars, so replace them when they get rusty. When screwing and securing the lid for general storage or for canning, it's advisable not to over tighten the metal bands, as this can sometimes warp and buckle the lids, breaking the seal. Speaking of seals, after the whole canning process, you may remove the bands once the jars have cooled down to room temperature. Removing the band saves it from being in contact with moisture for a really long time, and it will be easier for you to inspect any breaks in the seal.

• The key problem that we are trying to prevent in canning is botulism. The Clostridium botulinum bacteria really loves the low-oxygen and moist environment that comes when storing food in jars. When they proliferate, they release toxins that are harmful and even fatal to humans. The things that can kill them are heat and acidity. That is why sterilization is important, particularly for meat and non-acidic recipes. A quick blast of heat in the water bath or steam canner at 212°F will kill other harmful microorganisms in acidic food, but for botulism, you will need temperatures over 212°F, hence the pressure canner. So, monitor those temperatures really well.

• When loading food into jars for general storage, just make sure that the jars are clean and dried well. For canning, however, the jars should be boiled for sterilization and kept warm. The sterilization for 10 minutes is to clean the jars, and they are kept warm since they will be processed after loading the food and closing the lids. Some home canners actually sterilize in their canning vessel, load the jars while inside the canning vessel (without spilling), adjust the water level, and seal it up for processing. That way, they are sure that there are not many opportunities for bacteria in the air to land into relatively cool jars.

• Cleaning the jar is quite easy - you just boil it really well. But for the lid, it gets a bit tricky. The lid has a sealant built into it, which is designed to melt a bit to connect seamlessly with the lip of your jar. So, if you boil the lid with the jar, it will not form a proper seal since the compound will be thoroughly melted.

The trick here is, after boiling the jars for 10 minutes at 212°F to sterilize, do not immediately remove them from the vessel. Give it about five minutes or so until the temperature cools down to 180°F. Quickly open the canner lid and drop in the jar lids and let them warm up until you are loading up your food. If you are pressure canning, however, there is no need to do this since the temperature above the boiling point will be enough to kill any bacteria.

• Speaking of sterilizing, when you start your boil, also include the tools that will come in contact with the food and the jars into the boil or steam, except for the lids, of course. These should include the funnel, jar lifters, large spoons, ladles, and the metal rings. Also, use the jar lifter as tongs when moving everything around or a gloved hand.

• After sealing your food, let the jars cool down to room temperature, and remove the metal rings. The hot air within the headspace of the jar should have contracted during the cooldown, creating a partial vacuum and keeping the lid in place. The sealing compound should have also done its job. Make a thorough inspection to see if there are any gaps, but do not turn the jar upside down.

The seal is still settling and will take a couple of days to completely re-harden. If there is a gap or the seal is broken just after the canning process, you can transfer the jar into your fridge after cooling to room temperature. It's still good to eat, but consume it within a week or so.

• Does the sterilization process feel like a lot of work? Don't worry about it. It's only necessary if the canning process is below 10 minutes or so. A canning process over 10 minutes is enough time to kill any bacteria, and it's also not necessary for short-term or general storage. The jars will still have to be properly cleaned, obviously.

• For general storage, you can go nuts and play around with the recipes I have included here. However, for canning recipes, please do follow the recipes as much as you can, particularly the canning process, temperature and time. Canning recipes are formulated, tested, and approved by laboratories and government institutions to ensure safety. The canning recipes I have included in this book were approved by the USDA, NCHFP, and their affiliated organizations.

• A common phrase and principle among home canners, home fermenters, and home charcutiers alike is "if in doubt, throw it out." In home canning, there will always be instances where you will encounter something odd with your work. It can be odd stuff on the surface, an odd smell, or an odd color. With something like botulism at stake, it's best to just throw that particular jar's contents out instead of risking it and eating the stuff. Keep in mind that inside the can is a nutrient-rich, low oxygen, and really moist environment, which is good breeding ground for some really nasty stuff. So be careful, and make informed judgments.

# 7 Jump, Jar Jar!

Going through all these recipes might be jarring for you, but I hope that I have taught you about meal prepping, meal canning, and food management in general. The world whizzes by really fast nowadays with all the things going on in our lives, and we miss a lot of the important things. Slowing down is a luxury that very few can afford. Instead, we have to keep up with life and somehow manage to take in the important bits along the way.

The simple act of preparing meals with your family, or

just for yourself, during the weekends is a good way to center and balance yourself by spending some time with your family or doing something simple that you can actually enjoy. At the same time, you are preparing for the week ahead, and even for the week after that, all while setting yourself up to bear that Monday-to-Friday grind without worrying about your next meal.

Making your meals also sets you up for healthy eating habits, despite the usual office stress. Hey, it can also give you something to look forward to since you are eating on a schedule. By practicing proper portioning and mixing things up a bit, you can improve your diet and be healthy even if you don't have the time to exercise.

You will also be a great asset to the environment and to local businesses by eating what is local and in season. This cuts your carbon footprint and helps small-time producers directly, showing fellowship in the community. You also cut back on food waste and misuse of your food budget by eating fresh and preserving the rest. This may be a simple meal-prepping skill, but it has an impact on several aspects of your life.

I know that times are tough all around, but we should

still strive to make something that truly matters. Don't let life pass you by. You should enjoy it. Eat healthy, and be healthy. While you're at it, lessen your food waste, develop a hobby that will sustain you through your life, and save some cash along the way. Making meals in jars is good for you and good for the planet. Keep at it, and soon, these hard times will soon be a thing of the past!

Made in United States
Orlando, FL
16 September 2024

51576843R00091